*"Anyone who stops learning is old, whether at twenty or eighty. Anyone who keeps learning stays young."*

HENRY FORD

ISBN: 9798340625175
Imprint: Independently published

This book has been crafted with the assistance of AI technology to help provide clear explanations and engaging examples. While every effort has been made to ensure the accuracy and enjoyment of the content, readers should note that AI-generated suggestions are always subject to review, and human insight remains an essential part of the creative process. We hope this book serves as a helpful guide in your journey

# Contents

# INTRODUCTION

Welcome to "Your First Android Phone: An Essential Guide for Seniors." This book is designed with you in mind, whether you're completely new to smartphones or just looking to get more comfortable with your Android device. Today's phones offer so many wonderful features—keeping in touch with family, taking pictures, browsing the internet, and even managing your health—all from the palm of your hand.

We understand that learning new technology can feel overwhelming, especially when devices seem complex. That's why this guide takes a step-by-step approach, explaining everything in clear and simple terms. We've included detailed instructions, helpful tips, and illustrations where possible to make sure you feel confident using your Android phone.

Throughout this guide, you'll discover:

**How to make and receive calls**—staying connected with family and friends has never been easier.

**Sending text messages and emails**—learn how to share updates, photos, and more with loved ones.

**Exploring apps**—from health and fitness to entertainment and games, there's something for everyone.

**Customizing your phone**—make your phone work for you with personalized settings and accessibility features.

**Staying safe and secure**—learn how to protect your personal information and avoid common pitfalls.

This book has been designed for seniors, but anyone who feels unsure or intimidated by new technology will benefit from the straightforward guidance and practical tips it offers. With this guide in hand, you'll be able to use your Android phone with confidence, and soon enough, it will become a valuable tool in your daily life.

So, whether you're using your Android phone to keep in touch with loved ones, organize your day, or explore new apps and services, we hope this book empowers you to get the most out of your device. Happy learning and welcome to the wonderful world of Android!.

# CHAPTER 1: INTRODUCTION TO ANDROID PHONES AND THE ANDROID OPERATING SYSTEM

## What is Android?

At its core, Android is an operating system (OS) developed by **Google**, designed specifically for touchscreen devices like smartphones and tablets. It is one of the most popular operating systems in the world, powering over **2.5 billion devices** globally. Android provides the interface that allows you to interact with your phone, use apps, and control features like Wi-Fi, Bluetooth, the camera, and more.

Unlike Apple's iOS, which only runs on Apple devices like the iPhone, Android is an open-source operating system. This means that it is used by many different phone manufacturers, including Samsung, Google (Pixel), Motorola, Huawei, LG, OnePlus, and more. This openness allows for a wider range of devices with varying price points, features, and styles, so users can choose a phone that best suits their needs and budget.

### Understanding the Android Operating System

Android is a powerful and flexible operating system that allows your phone to run multiple apps, connect to the internet, take pictures, play music, and much more. Here are a few key components of the Android operating system that you'll encounter as you use your phone:

- **User Interface (UI):** This is what you see and interact with on the screen. Android's UI includes features like the home screen, app drawer, notification panel, and widgets. Different manufacturers might customize the UI, which is why a Samsung phone might look slightly different from a Google Pixel phone.

- **Home Screen and App Drawer:** When you unlock your phone, you land on the home screen. Here, you can place shortcuts to your favourite apps, add widgets, and more. The app drawer is where all your installed apps are listed.

- **Google Play Store:** One of Android's most valuable components is the Google Play Store, which allows you to download and install apps for everything from social media to health tracking. This ecosystem is huge, with over 3 million apps available.

- **Android Versions:** Google regularly updates Android to provide new features and security improvements. These updates come with a version number, and each major release is often named after a dessert (e.g., Android Pie, Android Oreo). The most recent versions, however, have adopted a number-only naming convention (e.g., Android 12, Android 13).

- **Customization:** One of the best aspects of Android is its customizability. Unlike iOS, Android allows you to personalize your device extensively, from changing the layout of your home screen to installing launchers (apps that change the look and feel of your phone's interface) or adding widgets that provide at-a-glance information like weather or news updates.

## Types of Android Phones

Since many companies manufacture Android phones, they come in a wide variety of sizes, shapes, and specifications. Here's a breakdown of the major types of Android phones:

1. **Flagship Android Phones**: These are premium devices with the latest technology, features, and performance. Examples include:
   - **Samsung Galaxy S** series (e.g., Galaxy S23): Known for their top-of-the-line screens, powerful cameras, and fast processors.
   - **Google Pixel series** (e.g., Pixel 8): Known for its clean, minimal Android experience and AI-powered features like advanced photography.

2. **Mid-range Android Phones**: These devices offer good performance at a more affordable price point. Examples include:
   - **Samsung Galaxy A series**: Offers solid performance and features at a lower price than the flagship models.
   - **OnePlus Nord:** Known for its fast performance and sleek design while being more affordable than flagship devices.

3. **Budget Android Phones**: These phones provide essential smartphone functionality at an entry-level price, making them ideal for first-time smartphone users or those looking for a more basic device. Examples include:
   - **Moto G series**: Affordable, reliable devices with basic features for everyday use.
   - **Xiaomi Redmi series**: Known for providing good features at an extremely competitive price.

## How Does Android Compare to Other Operating Systems?

It's important to understand how Android differs from other mobile operating systems like iOS (Apple's iPhone OS). Here's a quick comparison:

- **Flexibility and Customization**: Android allows users to customize their phones in ways that iOS does not. You can change the look of your home screen, install alternative apps for basic functions (e.g., browsers, messaging), and even modify system settings more freely.

- **Device Options**: Since Android is used by multiple manufacturers, there are far more devices to choose from, at varying price points. This means that no matter your budget, there's likely an Android phone available that suits your needs.

- **App Stores:** Both iOS and Android have vast app ecosystems, but Android offers more apps due to its open nature. However, this also means that Android users need to be more careful about the apps they download, as Google Play Store has more flexibility for developers, which can sometimes result in malicious apps being present.

- **Updates:** Apple provides faster and more universal updates to its iPhones, whereas Android updates can sometimes be delayed depending on the manufacturer and carrier. For example, Google Pixel devices receive updates directly from Google, while Samsung users may experience a slight delay.

## Why Choose an Android Phone?

For seniors, Android phones offer several advantages:

1. **Variety of Devices**: Android offers a wide range of devices, allowing you to choose based on your budget, screen size preferences, and desired features. If you want a large screen with a high-resolution display, you can opt for a flagship device like the Samsung Galaxy S series. If you prefer something smaller and more affordable, you can choose from various mid-range or budget models.

2. **Customization:** Android phones are highly customizable, which means you can adjust the layout, fonts, and even system settings to make your phone easier to use. You can install a custom launcher to simplify the interface, which is especially helpful if you prefer a simpler, more senior-friendly experience.

3. **Widgets and Shortcuts**: Widgets are small apps that run directly on your home screen, allowing you to quickly

access important information like weather updates, news, or your calendar. You can also set up shortcuts to call or message your most important contacts directly from your home screen.

4. **Google Integration:** If you already use Google services like Gmail, Google Photos, or Google Maps, an Android phone will seamlessly integrate with your Google account. This means your emails, photos, contacts, and other important data are always synced across all your devices.

5. **Affordability:** Android offers a wider range of pricing options, making it easier to find a phone that fits within your budget. Whether you're looking for an affordable, entry-level device or a high-end flagship, Android has an option for you.

## Key Features of Android Phones

While the exact features of an Android phone may vary depending on the manufacturer, here are some common features that most Android phones include:

- **Touchscreen Interface**: Almost all modern Android phones feature a touchscreen, allowing you to interact with apps and menus by tapping, swiping, and pinching.

- **Camera:** Android phones are known for their powerful cameras, which allow you to take high-quality photos and videos. Many models include multiple lenses, such as wide-angle and zoom lenses, for capturing different types of shots.

- **Internet Access**: Android phones can connect to the internet via Wi-Fi or mobile data (from your phone carrier). This allows you to browse websites, watch videos, download apps, and more.

- **GPS and Google Maps**: With built-in GPS, Android phones can give you real-time navigation and location-based services through apps like Google Maps.

- **App Integration:** Whether it's checking your email,

listening to music, tracking your fitness, or keeping in touch with loved ones, Android phones offer seamless app integration to enhance your everyday life.

## The Android Ecosystem: More Than Just Phones

Android isn't just limited to smartphones. Google has built an entire ecosystem around the Android platform, including tablets, smartwatches, smart speakers, and even smart TVs. Many Android devices can work together to provide a seamless experience across different devices. For instance, your Android phone can connect to a Google Nest smart speaker, allowing you to control your smart home devices using voice commands through Google Assistant.

## Your Journey with Android

In this guide, we'll be walking you through everything you need to know about using your Android phone, from setting it up to making calls, sending messages, downloading apps, and even customizing it to your liking. By the end of this guide, you'll feel confident in navigating the Android operating system and using your phone to stay connected with friends, family, and the world around you.

In the next chapter, we'll start by taking you through the setup process for your new Android phone, ensuring that everything is configured exactly how you need it.

# CHAPTER 2: SETTING UP YOUR ANDROID PHONE

Setting up your Android phone for the first time is an exciting experience, but it can feel overwhelming if you're new to smartphones. Don't worry—this chapter will guide you through every step of the process, from turning on the phone to customizing key settings, ensuring that your phone is set up to fit your personal preferences and needs.

## 1. Unboxing and Turning On Your Phone

Before we get started, make sure you have all the essentials. In the box, you should find:

- The Android phone itself
- A charging cable and plug adapter
- Instructions or a quick-start guide
- A SIM card (depending on your carrier)

Once you've unboxed the phone, follow these steps:

- **Charging Your Phone**: If your phone isn't fully charged, plug it into the charger and give it some time to charge before starting the setup process.

- **Inserting the SIM Card**: If your phone requires a SIM card, follow the instructions provided in the box or ask your carrier for assistance. The SIM card allows you to make calls, send texts, and use mobile data.

- **Powering On**: Hold down the Power button (usually

located on the side of the phone) until the screen turns on. You'll see the manufacturer's logo (e.g., Samsung, Google, or Motorola) as the phone boots up.

## 2. Choosing Your Language

The first thing you'll be prompted to do is select your preferred language. This is the language in which all the menus, instructions, and apps will appear on your phone.

- Scroll through the list of languages and tap the one you want. For example, if you prefer English, tap "English (United States)" or whichever variation of English suits you.
- Once you select the language, tap Next to continue.

**Tip:** Don't worry if you accidentally choose the wrong language—you can change it later in the settings.

## 3. Connecting to Wi-Fi

To get the most out of your Android phone, you'll need an internet connection. If you're at home or in a place with Wi-Fi, now is the time to connect. Follow these steps:

- Select Your Wi-Fi Network: The phone will automatically search for nearby Wi-Fi networks. Choose your network from the list.
- Enter the Wi-Fi Password: If the network is secured, you'll need to enter the password. If you don't know the password, check your router, or ask the person who set up your Wi-Fi.
- Tap Connect: Once you've entered the correct password, tap Connect. Your phone will now be connected to the internet, allowing you to download updates, apps, and other important features.

**Tip:** If you don't have Wi-Fi at the moment, you can skip this step and connect later.

## 4. Signing into Your Google Account

Your Google account is essential for accessing many of the key features of your Android phone, including the Google Play Store, Gmail, Google Photos, and Google Drive. If you don't have a Google account, you can create one during this step.

- **Sign in with an Existing Account**: If you already have a Google account (for example, if you've used Gmail or YouTube before), enter your email address and password to sign in.

- **Create a New Google Account**: If you don't have an account, tap Create Account and follow the prompts to set one up. You'll need to enter your name, choose a username (which will also be your email address), and create a password.

- **Syncing Your Data:** Once you sign in, your phone will give you the option to sync your Google account data. This includes contacts, emails, calendar events, and app data if you're restoring from an old phone. If you want your data to be synced automatically, make sure the Sync option is enabled.

**Tip:** If you don't want to sign in with a Google account, you can skip this step. However, some services (like downloading apps from the Play Store) will require a Google account.

## 5. Setting Up Security: PIN, Password, or Fingerprint

One of the most important steps in setting up your phone is ensuring it's secure. Android phones offer several ways to protect your phone from unauthorized access, including PIN codes, passwords, patterns, and even fingerprint or face recognition.

- **PIN or Password:** You'll be prompted to create a PIN or password to unlock your phone. A PIN is usually a 4-6 digit number, while a password can include both letters and numbers. Choose something easy for you to remember but difficult for others to guess.

- **Fingerprint or Face Recognition:** Many Android phones have a fingerprint scanner or facial recognition feature for added security. If your phone has these options, you'll be asked if you want to set them up. You can follow the on-screen instructions to scan your fingerprint or face.

**Tip:** Even if you choose to use fingerprint or face recognition, you'll still need a backup PIN or password in case the other methods fail.

## 6. Updating Your Phone

Once your phone is connected to the internet, it may check for software updates. It's a good idea to install these updates, as they often include important security patches and new features.

- **Check for Updates**: If an update is available, your phone will notify you and give you the option to install it immediately or later. If you choose to install now, follow the on-screen instructions, and the phone will restart after the update is complete.

**Tip:** Make sure your phone is connected to Wi-Fi and is either fully charged or plugged into a charger when updating, as updates can take a while to download and install.

## 7. Setting Up Additional Preferences

After setting up security and updating your phone, you'll be guided through additional preferences that help customize your phone to your needs. Some of these options include:

- **Google Assistant:** Google Assistant is a voice-activated virtual assistant that can help you make calls, set reminders, check the weather, and more. You'll be asked if you want to enable Google Assistant during setup. If you agree, you can activate it later by saying "Hey Google."

- **Backup and Restore:** If you're switching from an old Android phone, you can restore your apps, contacts, and other data from a previous backup. Follow the prompts to restore from Google Drive if you have a backup saved.

- **Location Services**: Location services allow apps like

Google Maps to access your phone's GPS to provide location-based information. You can turn this feature on or off during setup, but it's generally recommended to leave it on for apps that require it.

- **Customize Display and Font Size:** You'll have the option to adjust your phone's display size and text size. If you find the default text size too small, you can increase it to make it easier to read.

**Tip:** Don't worry if you skip a step or aren't sure about something. You can always change these settings later in the Settings menu.

## 8. Exploring the Home Screen and Apps

After completing the setup process, you'll be taken to the home screen. This is where you can access your most frequently used apps, adjust settings, and explore the features of your phone.

- **App Drawer:** To see all your apps, swipe up from the bottom of the screen to open the app drawer. Here you'll find pre-installed apps like the Phone, Messages, Contacts, Camera, and Settings apps.

- **Customize Your Home Screen:** You can rearrange apps, add widgets (like a clock or weather widget), and change your wallpaper to make your home screen feel personalized and organized.

## Conclusion

Setting up your Android phone is a straightforward process, and once you've completed these steps, you'll be ready to start exploring all the features your phone has to offer. Whether it's sending messages, taking photos, or downloading new apps, your phone is now set up to help you stay connected and make your daily tasks easier. Take your time, explore the settings, and customize your phone to suit your personal preferences.

# CHAPTER 3: GETTING TO KNOW YOUR HOME SCREEN

The home screen is the central hub of your Android phone —it's where you access your favourite apps, check important notifications, and customize your device to suit your needs. Learning how to navigate and personalize the home screen will make your phone more efficient and user-friendly. In this chapter, we'll explore the key elements of the home screen and how you can make it work for you.

## 1. Understanding the Home Screen Layout

The home screen is the first thing you see when you unlock your phone, and it's designed to be a user-friendly space where you can quickly access the most important apps and information.

**Key Components of the Home Screen:**

- **App Icons:** These are the small images you tap to open apps. Common icons include the Phone, Messages, Contacts, and Camera apps. You can place your most frequently used apps on the home screen for easy access.

- **Dock:** At the bottom of the home screen, you'll find the dock, a row of app icons that remains the same no matter which page of the home screen you're on. This is a great place to store apps you use regularly, such as the Phone or Messages app.

- **Status Bar:** At the top of your screen is the status bar, which shows important information like the time, battery percentage, and Wi-Fi or mobile network signal strength. You'll also see small icons here that indicate notifications (e.g., new text messages or app updates).

- **Navigation Buttons:**
    - ◦ **Home Button:** This button, usually a circle icon, takes you back to the home screen no matter what app you're using.
    - ◦ **Back Button:** This button (often an arrow) allows you to go back to the previous screen or app.
    - ◦ **Recent Apps Button:** This button (usually a square or three lines) shows you the apps you've recently used and lets you quickly switch between them.

**Tip:** Some newer Android phones use gestures instead of buttons to navigate. For example, you might swipe up from the bottom of the screen to go back to the home screen.

## 2. Adding and Removing App Icons

The home screen is customizable, allowing you to add or remove app icons based on your preferences. You can arrange your apps in a way that makes sense for you, making frequently used apps easy to access.

### Adding Apps to the Home Screen:

- To add an app to your home screen, open the App Drawer (swipe up from the bottom of the screen or tap the icon with dots), find the app you want, and press and hold the app icon. After a second, your phone will vibrate slightly, and you can drag the app icon to the desired position on the home screen.

### Removing Apps from the Home Screen:

- If you want to remove an app from the home screen (without uninstalling it), press and hold the app icon until options appear, then drag it to the Remove or Trash icon at the top of the screen. This doesn't delete the app—it's still available in your app drawer.

**Tip:** Organize your home screen so that your most frequently used apps (like Phone, Messages, and Contacts) are easy to reach. Less frequently used apps can stay in the app drawer to avoid cluttering the home screen.

---

### 3. Creating Folders to Organize Your Apps

If you have a lot of apps on your home screen, creating folders can help you keep things organized. A folder groups similar apps together, so you don't have to scroll through multiple home screen pages to find what you need.

**How to Create a Folder:**

1. Press and hold an app icon you want to include in a folder.

2. Drag it onto another app icon that you'd like to group with it (for example, placing the Camera and Gallery apps together).

3. Once you drop the app on top of the other, a folder will automatically be created.

4. You can rename the folder by tapping on the text box that appears above it and typing in a new name (e.g., "Social" for messaging and social media apps or "Games" for your entertainment apps).

**Tip:** You can add more apps to an existing folder by dragging them into it. To remove an app from a folder, open the folder, press and hold the app icon, and drag it back to the home screen or app drawer.

---

### 4. Using Widgets on the Home Screen

Widgets are small, interactive tools that provide quick access to information or functions directly from the home screen. Common widgets include the clock, weather updates, calendar events, or a quick view of your emails or messages. Widgets save you time by displaying important information without needing to open an app.

**How to Add a Widget:**

1. Press and hold an empty space on the home screen until options appear.

2. Tap Widgets from the menu that pops up.

3. Browse through the available widgets (they're often grouped by the app they belong to, such as Google Calendar or Clock).

4. Press and hold the widget you want, then drag it to your home screen and place it where you like.

**Examples of Useful Widgets:**

- Clock Widget: Displays the time and date in a large format, making it easier to see at a glance.

- Weather Widget: Shows the current weather conditions and forecast for your area.

- Calendar Widget: Displays upcoming events or appointments from your Google Calendar.

- Google Search Widget: Allows you to quickly search the internet without needing to open a browser.

**Tip**: Some widgets are resizable. After placing the widget, you may be able to adjust its size by pressing and holding the widget and then dragging the edges.

## 5. Changing Your Wallpaper

Your Android phone allows you to customize the look of your home screen by changing the wallpaper (background image). You can choose from pre-installed images, use a photo from your gallery, or download a wallpaper from an app or website.

**How to Change Your Wallpaper:**

1. Press and hold an empty space on the home screen until options appear.

2. Tap Wallpapers from the menu.

3. You can choose from the phone's pre-installed wallpapers or select one from your photo gallery.

4. Tap Set Wallpaper to apply the image to your home screen.

**Tip:** You can choose different wallpapers for your lock screen and home screen, adding a personal touch to your phone. Try using a simple, uncluttered wallpaper on your home screen to make app icons easier to see.

## 6. Managing Notifications from the Home Screen

Notifications alert you when you receive a new message, an app update, or a calendar event. Managing notifications from the home screen can help you stay on top of important information without feeling overwhelmed.

**Checking Notifications:**

- When you receive a new notification, a small icon will appear in the status bar at the top of the screen. To see more details, swipe down from the top of the screen to open the Notification Shade. Here, you can read and interact with notifications, such as replying to a message or dismissing an alert.

**Dismissing Notifications:**

- If you don't want to deal with a notification right away, swipe it left or right to dismiss it.

**Managing Notification Settings:**

- If you find certain app notifications annoying or overwhelming, you can control which apps send you notifications. To do this:
    1. Go to Settings > Notifications.
    2. You'll see a list of apps and their notification preferences. Tap on an app to customize how and when you receive notifications from it.
    3. You can disable notifications for specific apps or customize how they appear (e.g., silent notifications or important notifications only).

**Tip:** Important notifications, such as messages or reminders, should remain enabled so you don't miss anything. Less important notifications (like those from games or promotional apps) can be turned off to reduce clutter.

## 7. Quick Settings Panel

The Quick Settings Panel gives you easy access to important functions like turning on Wi-Fi, adjusting brightness, or enabling

Airplane Mode. You can access it by swiping down from the top of the screen (either fully or with a two-finger swipe).

**Common Quick Settings Icons:**

- **Wi-Fi:** Toggle your Wi-Fi connection on or off.

- **Bluetooth:** Turn Bluetooth on or off if you use wireless headphones or connect to other devices.

- **Airplane Mode:** Disable all wireless communications when traveling on a plane.

- **Brightness Slider**: Adjust the brightness of your screen to a comfortable level.

- **Do Not Disturb:** Silence all notifications, calls, and alarms.

**Tip:** You can customize the Quick Settings panel by tapping the pencil icon or edit button (depending on your phone model). This allows you to add or remove shortcuts based on your preferences.

## Conclusion

The Android home screen is a powerful tool that you can customize to fit your needs. Whether it's organizing your apps, adding useful widgets, or managing notifications, your home screen can help you navigate your phone quickly and efficiently. Take your time to explore and personalize it, and soon you'll feel comfortable using your phone's home screen like a pro.

# CHAPTER 4: MAKING AND RECEIVING CALLS

At its core, your Android phone is a powerful communication tool, and making and receiving calls is one of its primary functions. While this might seem straightforward, Android phones offer a variety of features and settings that make phone calls more convenient, efficient, and personalized. Whether you're calling friends and family, managing contacts, or setting up voicemail, this chapter will walk you through the basics of handling calls on your Android phone and introduce you to some advanced features that can improve your calling experience.

## 1. Making a Phone Call

Making a phone call on an Android device is simple, but Android phones come in different shapes, sizes, and interfaces depending on the manufacturer (e.g., Samsung, Google Pixel, Motorola). Despite these differences, the steps to make a call are generally the same.

**How to Make a Phone Call:**

1. **Open the Phone App:** Look for the Phone app icon on your home screen or in your app drawer (typically represented by a green phone icon). Tap it to open the app.

2. **Access the Dial Pad:** If your phone app opens to recent calls or contacts, tap the Dial Pad icon (usually represented by a keypad icon) to manually dial a number.

3. **Enter the Phone Number**: Use the dial pad to enter the

phone number you want to call. If the person is saved in your contacts, you can start typing their name, and the contact will appear for easy selection.

4. **Tap the Call Button**: Once you've entered the number or selected the contact, tap the green Call button to initiate the call.

5. **End the Call**: When the call is complete, tap the End Call button (usually a red phone icon) to hang up.

**Tip:** If you frequently call certain people, consider adding them to your Favourites in the Phone app for quick access.

## 2. Receiving a Phone Call

When you receive a phone call, your Android phone will ring, and a call screen will appear. Depending on your phone's settings and model, you'll have several options for answering or dismissing the call.

**How to Receive a Call:**

1. **Swipe to Answer:** When a call comes in, swipe the Phone icon from the bottom of the screen to the top (on some devices, swipe right) to answer the call.

2. **Dismiss or Reject a Call:** If you don't want to answer the call, swipe the Red Decline icon (or swipe left, depending on the model). The caller will either be sent to voicemail or hear a busy tone.

3. **Send a Quick Message:** If you're unable to answer but want to acknowledge the call, swipe up on the Message icon to send a pre-written text, such as "I'm busy, call you later."

**Tip:** Customize your quick response messages by going to Settings > Calls > Quick Responses, so you can personalize the texts you send when declining calls.

## 3. Using the Contacts App

Managing your contacts is key to making calls quickly and easily.

The Contacts app on Android allows you to save names, phone numbers, and additional information for easy access.

**How to Add a New Contact:**

1. **Open the Contacts App:** Look for the Contacts app on your home screen or in the app drawer (it may also be found inside the Phone app under a separate tab).
2. **Tap Add Contact:** Tap the Add (+) icon to create a new contact.
3. **Enter Contact Information:** Fill in the person's name, phone number, email address, and any other relevant information (such as a birthday or address).
4. **Save the Contact**: Once you've entered the necessary information, tap Save.

**How to Call a Contact:**

1. **Open the Contacts App:** Navigate to the Contacts app.
2. **Find the Contact:** Scroll through your list or use the search bar at the top to find the contact you want to call.
3. **Tap the Phone Icon:** Once you've found the contact, tap the Phone icon next to their name to place a call.

**Tip:** You can also access contacts by typing their name in the search bar of the Phone app.

---

### 4. Managing Missed Calls and Voicemail

Missing a call doesn't mean missing the opportunity to stay connected. Android phones have built-in systems for managing missed calls and voicemail, allowing you to follow up on missed communications at your convenience.

**How to View Missed Calls:**

1. **Open the Phone App:** Missed calls are often highlighted at the top of the call log in the Phone app.
2. **Check the Call Log:** Scroll through the Recents tab to view your missed calls. The call log will show the caller's name or number, the time of the missed call, and

whether they left a voicemail.

**How to Set Up Voicemail:**

1. **Open the Phone App:** Tap the Phone app icon.

2. **Access Voicemail Settings:** Tap the three-dot menu (or More icon) in the corner of the screen and select Settings. Then tap Voicemail.

3. **Set Up Your Greeting:** Follow the on-screen prompts to set up your voicemail greeting and access number (your phone may come with a default voicemail setup from your carrier).

4. **Access Voicemails**: When you receive a voicemail, you'll get a notification. Tap the notification to listen to the message or dial into your voicemail by holding down the 1 key on the dial pad.

**Tip:** You can adjust voicemail settings, including greeting options, notification settings, and voicemail-to-text services if supported by your carrier.

---

## 5. Call Settings and Features

Android phones come with a variety of call settings and features that can make your calling experience more efficient and enjoyable.

**Key Call Features:**

- **Call Waiting:** This feature alerts you if someone tries to call while you're already on a call. You can choose to switch between calls or merge them.

- **Call Forwarding:** Allows you to forward incoming calls to another phone number when you're unavailable. To set up call forwarding, go to Settings > Calls > Call Forwarding.

- **Do Not Disturb (DND):** When you need peace and quiet, you can activate Do Not Disturb, which blocks incoming calls and notifications. However, you can set exceptions to allow certain contacts to call through.

1. Go to Settings > Sound > Do Not Disturb.

2. Choose Allow Exceptions and select contacts whose calls will come through even in DND mode.

- **Caller ID & Spam Protection:** Some Android devices come with built-in caller ID and spam detection. It alerts you if a call is likely spam and can block unwanted numbers.

   1. Go to Phone app > Settings > Caller ID & Spam and enable Filter Spam Calls.

**Tip:** Explore your phone's Call Settings menu to see more options, including blocking unknown numbers, voice call recording (if supported), and setting up specific ringtones for contacts.

---

## 6. Making International Calls

If you need to make an international call, Android makes the process straightforward. However, international calls can incur higher costs, so it's important to understand how to dial internationally and consider alternatives like using Wi-Fi calling or apps for free or low-cost international communication.

**How to Make an International Call:**

1. **Dial the Exit Code:** Start by dialing the exit code for your country (e.g., 011 for the U.S. or 00 for many European countries). You can use the "+" sign as well.

2. **Enter the Country Code:** After the exit code, enter the country code of the number you're calling (e.g., 44 for the UK or 91 for India).

3. **Dial the Phone Number:** Finally, dial the local phone number, excluding any leading zero in the number.

**Using Apps for International Calls:**

- WhatsApp and Skype allow free or low-cost international calls when connected to Wi-Fi or mobile data. These apps use the internet instead of traditional phone networks, reducing call costs, especially for long-distance communication.

**Tip:** Check with your carrier for international calling plans to avoid unexpected charges if you frequently make international calls.

---

### 7. Wi-Fi Calling

If your mobile signal is weak or unavailable but you have access to a Wi-Fi network, Wi-Fi calling allows you to make and receive calls using your Wi-Fi connection rather than relying on the cellular network.

### How to Enable Wi-Fi Calling:

1. **Open Settings:** Go to Settings > Connections or Settings > Network & Internet.
2. **Select Wi-Fi Calling:** Toggle the Wi-Fi Calling option on.
3. **Connect to Wi-Fi:** When Wi-Fi calling is enabled, your phone will automatically use Wi-Fi to make calls when the mobile signal is weak.

**Tip:** Wi-Fi calling is especially useful in areas with poor reception but strong Wi-Fi, such as basements, remote areas, or indoors where cellular signals struggle.

---

### Conclusion

Making and receiving calls on your Android phone is more than just dialing numbers. With features like call waiting, voicemail, Wi-Fi calling, and international call options, you can tailor your calling experience to suit your needs. Whether you're chatting with family across the country or checking in with a friend nearby, Android makes it easy to stay connected. As you explore these features, you'll discover that calling on Android is as versatile and user-friendly as the rest of the phone's capabilities

---

# CHAPTER 5: SENDING AND RECEIVING MESSAGES

Text messaging is one of the simplest and most convenient ways to communicate using your Android phone. Whether you're sending a quick update to a friend, sharing a photo, or engaging in a group conversation, the Messages app offers a wide range of features to keep you connected. In this chapter, we'll explore the basics of sending and receiving messages, as well as more advanced features like multimedia messaging, group chats, and even using voice dictation for easier typing.

## 1. Getting Familiar with the Messages App

The Messages app on your Android phone allows you to send text messages (SMS) and multimedia messages (MMS) to other mobile phones. It's usually represented by an icon that looks like a speech bubble or envelope and can be found on your home screen or in the app drawer.

**Main Sections of the Messages App:**

- **Conversations List:** When you open the Messages app, you'll see a list of recent conversations. Each conversation is displayed by the contact's name or phone number, along with a preview of the most recent message. If the message is unread, it will appear in bold.

- **New Message Icon:** This is usually represented by a "+" or pencil icon. Tapping it will allow you to start a new conversation or send a message to someone who is not yet in your contacts.

- **Search Bar:** Located at the top of the app, the search bar allows you to quickly find a contact or a specific message in one of your conversations. This can be very helpful if you want to look up old messages without scrolling through entire conversations.

**Tip:** You can tap and hold any conversation in the list to bring up options such as delete, archive, or mark as unread.

## 2. How to Send a Text Message

Sending a basic text message is simple, but there are several features that can make the process even more efficient.

### Steps to Send a Text Message:

1. **Open the Messages App:** Locate and open the Messages app on your home screen or in the app drawer.

2. **Start a New Conversation**: Tap the New Message icon (usually represented by a pencil or "+" icon).

3. **Select a Contact:**
   - If you're messaging someone from your contacts, start typing their name in the To field and select their contact when it appears.
   - If the person is not saved in your contacts, type their phone number manually in the To field.

4. **Type Your Message:** Tap the message box at the bottom of the screen and use the keyboard to type your message.

5. **Send the Message:** Once you've written your message, tap the Send icon (often a blue arrow or paper airplane) to send it.

**Tip:** If you want to add multiple recipients to your message, you can enter several names or numbers in the To field. This will create a group message (explained later in this chapter).

## 3. Sending Multimedia Messages (MMS)

Beyond basic text messages, Android phones allow you to send multimedia messages, which can include photos, videos, voice recordings, and even documents. These are referred to as MMS (Multimedia Messaging Service) messages.

## How to Send a Photo or Video:

1. **Open a Conversation:** Open an existing conversation or start a new one.

2. **Tap the Attach Icon:** Look for the paperclip or camera icon next to the message box.

3. **Choose a Photo or Video:**
   - **Camera:** If you want to take a new photo or video, tap the Camera icon and capture your image or video.
   - **Gallery:** To send an existing photo or video, tap the Gallery or Photo option and select the image or video from your phone's gallery.

4. **Send the Message:** Once the photo or video appears in the message box, tap the Send icon to send it.

Other Types of Multimedia You Can Send:

- **Audio Clips:** You can send voice recordings by tapping the microphone icon. Record your message and send it as an audio file.

- **Location:** Some phones allow you to share your current location by tapping the Location or Map icon.

- **Documents:** You can also send documents like PDFs or Word files by selecting the Attach or File option.

**Tip:** Be mindful that multimedia messages may require mobile data or Wi-Fi to send, and large files (like videos) may take longer to send depending on your connection.

## 4. Using Group Messaging

Group messaging allows you to send messages to multiple people at once, making it easier to plan events, share news, or keep in touch with family and friends.

## How to Start a Group Message:

1. Open the Messages App and tap the New Message icon.

2. Add Multiple Recipients: In the To field, type the names or numbers of everyone you want to include in the group message.

3. Write Your Message: Type your message in the text box as you would with any other message.

4. Send the Message: Tap the Send icon, and your message will be sent to everyone in the group.

**Things to Know About Group Messaging:**

- **Everyone Sees the Replies:** When someone replies to a group message, everyone in the group can see the reply. This makes it easy to keep track of conversations, but if privacy is important, consider sending individual messages instead.

- **Managing Group Chats:** Some phones allow you to mute group conversations if you don't want to receive constant notifications. You can usually find this option by tapping the three-dot menu in the group chat and selecting Mute or Notifications.

- **Leaving a Group Chat:** If you want to leave a group chat, go to the same three-dot menu and select Leave Conversation (depending on the phone and messaging app you are using).

**Tip:** Group messages are a great way to keep everyone on the same page for things like family gatherings, meetups, or sharing important updates.

## 5. Voice Dictation: An Easier Way to Type

If you find typing on the small screen of your phone difficult, you can use voice dictation to type messages by speaking. Your phone's keyboard has a built-in microphone that allows you to speak your message, and it will convert your speech into text.

**How to Use Voice Dictation:**

1. Open the Messages App and start a new message or open an existing conversation.

2. Tap the Microphone Icon: On your keyboard, you'll see a microphone icon. Tap it to activate voice dictation.

3. Speak Your Message: Speak clearly, and your words will appear in the message box. You can even say punctuation

marks (e.g., "Hi comma how are you question mark") to include punctuation.

4. **Edit If Needed:** After dictating your message, review it for any errors. You can make manual edits if the phone didn't capture your words correctly.

5. **Send the Message:** Tap the Send icon when you're ready.

**Tip:** Voice dictation is particularly helpful for those with limited mobility or anyone who prefers speaking over typing. It can also be faster than manually typing long messages.

## 6. Managing Conversations and Notifications

Over time, your Messages app may fill up with many conversations. It's important to know how to manage your conversations to keep the app organized and free of clutter.

**Archiving Conversations:**

- If you don't want to delete a conversation but want to remove it from your main screen, you can archive it. This hides the conversation from view but keeps it accessible in case you need it later.

- To archive a conversation, press and hold the conversation in the main list, then tap the archive icon (usually a box with a downward arrow).

**Deleting Conversations:**

- To delete a conversation, press and hold the conversation, then tap the delete option. This will permanently remove the conversation from your phone, so be sure you no longer need it before deleting.

**Muting Conversations:**

- If a specific conversation is generating too many notifications (for example, a group message), you can mute the conversation by tapping the three-dot menu in the conversation and selecting Mute or Notifications Off. This will stop notifications, but you'll still receive the messages.

**Customizing Message Notifications:**

- You can customize how and when your phone alerts you to new messages. Go to Settings > Notifications and adjust the settings for message notifications. You can choose to receive sound, vibration, or silent notifications based on your preference.

**Tip:** To reduce unnecessary notifications, consider muting or archiving group chats that aren't important to you.

## 7. Sending and Receiving International Messages

If you need to send a message to someone in another country, your Android phone supports international messaging. However, it's important to note that sending international messages may incur extra charges depending on your mobile carrier.

**Sending an International Message:**

- To send a message to an international number, you'll need to add the country code before the phone number. For example, to send a message to someone in the UK, you would add "+44" before the rest of the phone number.

**Tip:** Consider using internet-based messaging apps like WhatsApp or Facebook Messenger for international communication, as these apps allow you to send messages over Wi-Fi or mobile data without extra charges for international SMS.

## Conclusion

The Messages app on your Android phone offers more than just basic texting. By using multimedia messages, group chats, voice dictation, and customization options, you can tailor your messaging experience to fit your needs. Whether you're sharing photos with family, catching up with friends, or managing group conversations, messaging is a versatile and essential part of staying connected. Take your time to explore all the features available, and soon you'll be messaging like a pro.

# CHAPTER 6:
# MANAGING CONTACTS

Managing your contacts is essential for staying connected with friends, family, and important services. The Contacts app on your Android phone allows you to store and organize phone numbers, email addresses, and other details for people you communicate with regularly. In this chapter, we'll explore how to add, edit, delete, and organize your contacts, as well as how to sync contacts from different sources to ensure they are always up to date.

## 1. Adding a New Contact

Adding a new contact to your phone ensures that you always have easy access to the phone numbers and details of the people you communicate with most frequently. Here's how to add a contact to your Android phone:

**How to Add a Contact:**

1. **Open the Contacts App:** You can find the Contacts app on your home screen or in the app drawer (the icon usually looks like a person's silhouette).

2. **Tap the Add Contact Icon:** Look for the + or Add Contact icon, usually located at the bottom-right or top-right corner of the screen.

3. **Enter Contact Information:**
   - **Name:** Start by entering the person's name in the Name field.
   - **Phone Number: Tap the Phone field to enter their phone number. Be sure to include the area**

code.

- **Email Address (Optional): If you want to include an email address, tap the Email field and enter their address.**
- **Other Details (Optional): You can add additional information like their home address, birthday, or notes in the provided fields.**

4. **Tap** Save: Once you've entered all the necessary information, tap Save to add the contact to your list.

**Tip:** You can store multiple phone numbers and email addresses for the same contact (for example, a work and home phone number). Be sure to label each one clearly (e.g., "Work" or "Mobile") for easy reference.

## 2. Importing and Syncing Contacts

Many people have contacts stored across multiple platforms, such as Google, email accounts, or even on an old SIM card. Android phones make it easy to import contacts from various sources and sync them across devices, so you'll never lose important contact information.

**Importing Contacts from a SIM Card:** If you have contacts saved on an old SIM card, you can easily import them to your Android phone.

1. **Insert the SIM Card:** If your old SIM card contains your contacts, insert it into your phone.
2. **Open the Contacts App:** Go to the Contacts app.
3. **Tap the Menu Icon:** Look for the three-dot menu in the top-right corner and tap it.
4. **Select Import/Export:** Choose Import from SIM Card or a similar option, depending on your phone model.
5. **Select Contacts to Import:** Choose the contacts you want to transfer and tap Import.

**Syncing Contacts from Your Google Account:** If you have

contacts saved to your Google account (such as from Gmail or a previous Android phone), they can automatically sync to your phone.

1. **Go to Settings:** Open the Settings app on your phone.
2. **Select Accounts:** Tap Accounts or Users & Accounts.
3. **Choose Google:** Select your Google account.
4. **Turn on Sync:** Make sure the Contacts option is toggled on. Your phone will sync all contacts stored in your Google account.

**Tip:** Syncing your contacts with your Google account ensures that your contacts will be backed up and available on any device you log into with the same Google account.

## 3. Editing Contacts

Over time, people change phone numbers, email addresses, or other details. Editing a contact allows you to keep their information up to date.

**How to Edit a Contact:**

1. **Open the Contacts App:** Locate the Contacts app on your phone.
2. **Find the Contact to Edit:** Scroll through your contact list or use the Search bar at the top of the screen to find the contact.
3. **Tap the Contact:** Once you've found the contact, tap their name to open their details.
4. **Tap the Edit Icon:** Look for a pencil or Edit icon (usually at the top of the screen) and tap it.
5. **Make Your Changes:** Update the contact's phone number, email, or any other information that needs to be changed.
6. **Tap Save:** Once you've made your edits, tap Save to update the contact's information.

**Tip:** If a contact changes their name (for example, after getting married), be sure to update their contact details so you can easily find them in your list.

## 4. Deleting Contacts

If you no longer need a contact, you can remove them from your list to keep your contacts app organized. Deleting a contact is easy, but remember that once deleted, their information cannot be recovered unless you have synced contacts to your Google account or another backup service.

**How to Delete a Contact**:

1. **Open the Contacts App:** Find the Contacts app on your phone.
2. **Find the Contact to Delete:** Scroll through your contacts or use the Search bar to locate the person you want to remove.
3. **Tap the Contact:** Open the contact's details.
4. **Tap the Menu Icon:** Tap the three-dot menu in the top-right corner of the screen.
5. **Select Delete**: From the dropdown menu, choose Delete.
6. **Confirm Deletion:** A prompt will appear asking if you're sure you want to delete the contact. Tap Yes or Delete to confirm.

**Tip:** If you accidentally delete a contact, you can try restoring it from your Google account (if syncing was enabled) by going to your Google Contacts on a computer and checking the Trash folder.

## 5. Organizing Contacts

As your contact list grows, it can become more difficult to quickly find the people you need. Fortunately, Android phones provide several ways to organize and filter your contacts, making it easier to manage a large list.

**Creating Groups:** Grouping contacts allows you to organize your list by categories, such as Family, Friends, or Work Contacts.

1. **Open the Contacts App:** Go to the Contacts app.
2. **Tap the Menu Icon:** Tap the three-dot menu and select Groups or Labels (depending on your phone model).
3. **Create a New Group:** Tap Create Group or New Label and enter a name for the group (e.g., "Family" or "Work").
4. **Add Contacts to the Group:** Select the contacts you want to add to the group and tap Save.

**Using Contact Favourites:** If you frequently contact certain people, you can mark them as Favourites to quickly access their information.

1. **Open the Contacts App:** Go to the Contacts app.
2. **Find the Contact to Favourite:** Locate the contact you want to mark as a favourite.
3. **Tap the Star Icon:** Open the contact's details and tap the star icon at the top of the screen. The contact will now appear in your Favourites list for easy access.

**Tip:** Favourites will appear in a special section in the Phone app or Contacts app, so you can reach them quickly without searching through your full contact list.

---

### 6. Linking and Merging Duplicate Contacts

Sometimes, you might end up with duplicate contacts—perhaps because you imported contacts from multiple sources, such as your Google account and SIM card. Android phones allow you to link or merge duplicate contacts to streamline your list.

**How to Merge Duplicate Contacts:**

1. **Open the Contacts App:** Go to the Contacts app.
2. **Tap the Menu Icon:** Tap the three-dot menu and select Manage Contacts.
3. **Select Merge or Link Contacts:** Choose Merge Contacts or Link Contacts (depending on your phone model).
4. **Review Suggested Merges:** Your phone will display a list of contacts that may be duplicates. Review the

suggestions and select the ones you want to merge.

5. **Tap Merge:** Once you're satisfied with the selections, tap Merge to combine the duplicate contacts into one.

**Tip:** You can also manually merge contacts by opening one contact, tapping the menu icon, and selecting Link Contacts.

---

## 7. Backup and Restore Contacts

It's important to regularly back up your contacts so that they aren't lost if your phone is damaged, lost, or replaced. Your Android phone offers several ways to back up and restore contacts, ensuring that your information is always safe.

**Backing Up Contacts to Google:**

1. **Open the Contacts App:** Go to the Contacts app.

2. **Sync to Google Account:** Ensure that your contacts are syncing to your Google account by going to Settings > Accounts > Google and making sure the Contacts toggle is enabled.

3. **Automatic Backup:** Once synced, your contacts will automatically back up to your Google account. If you switch to a new phone, simply log in with the same Google account, and your contacts will be restored.

Exporting Contacts for Manual Backup: If you prefer to keep a manual backup of your contacts, you can export them to

---

# CHAPTER 7: EXPLORING THE CAMERA AND TAKING PHOTOS

One of the most exciting features of an Android phone is the camera. With just a tap, you can capture moments, snap selfies, and record videos to share with loved ones. Android phones come equipped with high-quality cameras that are easy to use for beginners but also offer advanced settings for those who want more control. In this chapter, we'll guide you through everything you need to know about using the camera, taking great photos, using advanced features, and managing your media.

## 1. Getting Started with the Camera App

Your Android phone's Camera app is easy to access and allows you to start snapping photos quickly. Here's how you can open the Camera app:

- **From the Home Screen:** Look for the Camera icon on your home screen or in the app drawer (the icon usually looks like a camera).
- **Quick Launch:** Some Android phones allow you to double-tap the Power button to quickly open the camera, even if your phone is locked.
- **Lock Screen Shortcut:** You can access the camera directly from your lock screen by swiping the Camera icon

(typically located in the bottom-right corner).

Once you open the camera, the screen will show the live viewfinder, which displays whatever the camera lens is pointing at.

## 2. Basic Camera Functions

The Camera app has several core functions that allow you to capture high-quality photos and videos easily.

- **Shutter Button:** The circular button at the bottom of the screen. Tap it to take a photo.
- **Switching Between Cameras:** Android phones typically have two cameras—one on the back (for taking photos of things in front of you) and one on the front (for taking selfies). Tap the camera switch icon (a circular arrow) to switch between the front and rear cameras.
- **Zoom:** Pinch the screen with two fingers to zoom in or out. Some phones also have a zoom slider on the screen for more precise control.
- **Flash:** The flash can help in low-light conditions. Tap the lightning bolt icon to turn the flash on, off, or set it to auto (the phone will decide when to use the flash based on the lighting).
- **Viewfinder Grid:** Some Android phones offer a grid overlay in the viewfinder that helps you align your shots. This is useful for ensuring the horizon is level or for applying photography techniques like the rule of thirds.

**Tip:** Make sure your phone is stable when taking a photo to avoid blurry pictures. You can rest your elbows on a table or use both hands to hold the phone.

## 3. Taking Great Photos

While the camera is easy to use, there are a few tips that can help you take even better photos.

**Focus on the Subject:**

- Tap on the screen where you want the camera to focus. The camera will adjust its focus to that spot, making sure the subject is sharp and clear. For example, if you're taking a picture of a person, tap on their face to focus on them.

**Using Natural Light:**

- Natural light can dramatically improve your photos. Try taking pictures near a window or outside to make use of sunlight. If the lighting is too dim, your phone will likely use the flash, but natural light tends to produce the best results.

**Framing the Shot:**

- Consider how the subject is framed in the shot. The rule of thirds is a basic photography principle: imagine the screen is divided into three equal parts horizontally and vertically, and place the most important parts of the image along these lines for a more balanced composition.

**Take Multiple Shots:**

- Don't hesitate to take multiple photos of the same subject. You can always delete extras later, but having more options increases the likelihood of getting the perfect shot.

---

## 4. Advanced Camera Features

Android phones offer many advanced features for photography enthusiasts or anyone looking to experiment with their camera settings.

**Portrait Mode:**

- Portrait mode is great for taking photos of people or pets. It blurs the background, making the subject stand out. On many Android phones, you can activate Portrait mode by swiping through the camera modes (usually labelled Portrait or Live Focus).

**Night Mode:**

- Night mode is designed to help you take better photos in low-light situations, such as during the evening or in a dimly lit room. When enabled, Night mode uses longer exposure times to capture more light and produce a clearer image.

**HDR (High Dynamic Range):**

- HDR automatically takes several photos at different exposure levels and combines them to create a single image with better detail in both bright and dark areas. It's great for capturing scenes with strong contrasts, like a sunset. HDR is often enabled automatically in modern phones, but you can also turn it on manually in the settings.

**Panorama Mode:**

- Panorama mode allows you to take wide, sweeping photos of landscapes or large group shots. In this mode, you slowly move the phone from one side to the other while the camera captures a wide view.

**Pro Mode:**

- If you want full control over the camera's settings, Pro Mode lets you manually adjust things like shutter speed, ISO (light sensitivity), white balance, and focus. This mode is ideal for more experienced photographers or if you're looking to learn more about photography.

**Filters and Effects:**

- Many phones offer built-in filters and effects that you can apply while taking a photo. These can be fun for enhancing colours or adding creative effects to your pictures.

## 5. Taking and Editing Videos

In addition to taking photos, your Android phone can also record high-quality videos. The Video mode in the Camera app allows you to capture moments in motion, whether you're recording a family event, capturing the beauty of nature, or filming a tutorial.

**How to Record a Video:**

1. **Switch to Video Mode:** In the Camera app, swipe to the Video option or tap the Video icon (usually a red circle).
2. **Start Recording:** Tap the red record button to start recording. While recording, you can tap the screen to refocus on different areas of the video.
3. **Stop Recording:** Tap the red stop button to finish recording.
4. **Review the Video:** You can view the video by tapping the thumbnail that appears in the corner after you stop recording.

**Editing Videos:**

- You can trim, cut, or apply filters to your videos directly in the Gallery app. Tap the video, then look for the Edit option. You can drag the sliders at the start and end of the video to trim unwanted parts.

**Slow Motion and Time-Lapse:**

- Many Android phones come with special video modes like Slow Motion (which captures fast-moving objects in slow motion) and Time-Lapse (which speeds up long periods of time into a short video). These modes can add a creative touch to your videos.

---

**6. Managing and Organizing Photos and Videos**

After capturing photos and videos, you'll want to know where to find and manage them. Your Android phone saves all your media in the Gallery or Photos app, where you can view, edit, and organize them.

**How to Access Your Photos and Videos:**

- Open the Gallery app (or Google Photos, depending on your phone model). You'll see your photos and videos arranged in albums (e.g., Camera, Screenshots,

Downloads).

**Editing Photos:**

- Android phones have basic editing tools that allow you to enhance your photos directly in the Gallery app. Some common editing options include:
  - **Crop:** Remove unwanted parts of the photo.
  - **Rotate:** Adjust the orientation of the photo.
  - **Filters:** Apply preset filters to change the mood or colour tone of the photo.
  - **Brightness and Contrast:** Adjust the lighting and shadows to improve the overall look of the photo.

**Organizing Photos into Albums:**

- You can create albums to organize your photos by category (e.g., Vacations, Family).
  1. Open the Gallery app.
  2. Select the photos you want to move into an album.
  3. Tap the three-dot menu and select Create Album or Move to Album.

**Backing Up Your Photos and Videos:**

- It's a good idea to back up your photos and videos to ensure they aren't lost if your phone is damaged or replaced. You can back them up using Google Photos:
  1. **Open Google Photos:** If it's not already installed, download it from the Google Play Store.
  2. **Enable Backup:** Tap your profile icon (top-right corner), then select Photos Settings > Back up & sync. This will automatically back up all your photos and videos to your Google account.
  3. **Access Your Photos from Anywhere:** Once backed up, you can access your photos from any device by logging into your Google account.

## 7. Sharing Your Photos and Videos

After capturing and editing your photos and videos, you'll likely want to share them with friends and family. Android phones make it easy to share media through messages, social media apps, or email.

### Sharing via Messages:

1. Open the Gallery app and select the photo or video you want to share.
2. Tap the Share icon (usually three connected dots or lines).
3. Select Messages and choose the contact you want to send the photo or video to.

### Sharing via Social Media:

- You can also share photos directly to social media platforms like Facebook, Instagram, or WhatsApp by selecting the Share icon and choosing the app.

**Tip:** For large files (like long videos), consider using cloud services like Google Drive or Dropbox to share links rather than sending the entire file.

## Conclusion

Your Android phone's camera is a powerful tool for capturing memories, whether through photos or videos. By mastering the basic functions and experimenting with advanced features like portrait mode, night mode, and video editing, you can take professional-looking pictures and videos with ease. Don't forget to back up your photos and videos, so they are always safe and accessible. With the tips and techniques in this chapter, you're well on your way to becoming a confident and creative smartphone photographer.

# CHAPTER 8: CONNECTING TO THE INTERNET AND BROWSING THE WEB

The internet is a vast source of information, entertainment, and communication, and your Android phone makes it easy to access. Whether you want to check the news, shop online, search for information, or watch videos, the internet is at your fingertips. In this chapter, we'll cover how to connect to the internet, use a web browser, and ensure a safe and enjoyable browsing experience.

## 1. Connecting to the Internet

Before you can browse the web, you'll need to ensure your phone is connected to the internet. You can connect either via Wi-Fi or your mobile data. Using Wi-Fi is often preferable when you're at home or in a public space with Wi-Fi access, as it's usually faster and doesn't consume your mobile data.

**Connecting to Wi-Fi:**

1. **Open the Settings App:** Swipe down from the top of the screen to open the notification panel, then tap the gear icon to open the Settings app.

2. **Select Wi-Fi:** Tap Wi-Fi in the settings menu.

3. **Choose a Network:** Your phone will display a list of available Wi-Fi networks. Tap the one you want to connect to.

4. **Enter the Password:** If the network is password-protected, you'll need to enter the password. Then, tap Connect.

Once connected, you'll see a Wi-Fi symbol in the status bar at the top of your screen.

**Using Mobile Data:** If you're not near a Wi-Fi network, you can use your phone's mobile data to access the internet. Your phone should automatically connect to mobile data when Wi-Fi is unavailable.

To check if mobile data is enabled:

1. **Open Settings:** Go to Settings > Connections > Mobile Data.
2. **Enable Mobile Data:** Toggle the switch to On.

**Tip:** Using mobile data may incur additional charges depending on your mobile plan, so it's best to connect to Wi-Fi whenever possible, especially when streaming videos or downloading large files.

## 2. Using a Web Browser

Your Android phone comes with a built-in web browser, typically Google Chrome, although some devices may use a different browser like Samsung Internet. The web browser allows you to visit websites, search for information, and access online services.

**How to Open the Browser:**

1. **Find the Browser Icon:** Look for the Chrome or Internet icon on your home screen or in the app drawer.
2. **Tap to Open:** Tap the icon to open the browser.

**The Browser Interface:**

- **Address/Search Bar:** At the top of the screen is the address bar. You can type a web address (URL) here, such as www.google.com, or enter search terms to find information.
- **Tabs:** You can open multiple websites at once by using

tabs. To open a new tab, tap the plus (+) icon at the top of the screen. You can switch between open tabs by tapping the tab icon (usually a small square with a number).

- **Menu:** The three-dot menu in the upper-right corner offers additional options, such as opening a new tab, accessing bookmarks, or viewing your browsing history.

## 3. Searching the Web

You don't need to know the exact web address of a site to find information online. Simply type your search terms into the browser's address bar, and it will return a list of relevant results.

**How to Perform a Web Search:**

1. **Open the Browser:** Launch Chrome or your preferred browser.
2. **Type Your Search:** In the address bar, type what you're looking for. For example, "local weather," "best restaurants near me," or "how to change my password."
3. **Press Enter:** Tap the search icon (magnifying glass) or the Go/Enter button on your keyboard.
4. **View Results:** The browser will display a list of search results. Tap a result to visit the website.

**Tip:** You can use search engines like Google, Bing, or DuckDuckGo to find the information you need. Google is the default search engine on most Android phones.

## 4. Navigating Websites

Once you've opened a website, you can browse and interact with the content. Here's how to navigate a webpage:

- **Scroll:** Use your finger to scroll up or down the page. You can also swipe left or right if the content allows it.
- **Links:** Tap links (usually underlined or in a different colour) to visit other pages or sections of the website.
- **Back and Forward:** Use the back arrow at the bottom or top of the screen to return to the previous page, or tap the

forward arrow to go back to a page you left.

- **Refreshing a Page:** If a page isn't loading properly or you want to see the latest content, tap the refresh icon (a circular arrow) in the browser's toolbar.

**Tip:** Be cautious when clicking on links in unfamiliar websites, as they could lead to spam or malicious sites. Always ensure the website is secure (look for "https" in the URL or a padlock icon next to the address).

## 5. Using Bookmarks and Saving Pages

If you visit certain websites regularly, you can bookmark them to access them more quickly.

### How to Bookmark a Website:

1. **Open the Website**: Go to the page you want to bookmark.
2. **Tap the Menu Icon:** In the top-right corner of the browser (usually three dots), tap the menu icon.
3. **Select Add to Bookmarks:** Tap Add to Bookmarks or Bookmark this Page. This will save the page for easy access later.

### Accessing Bookmarks:

- To view your saved bookmarks, open the browser, tap the menu icon, and select Bookmarks. You'll see a list of all the pages you've saved.

### Saving Pages for Offline Viewing:

- If you want to view a webpage later without an internet connection, you can save it for offline viewing.
    1. Open the webpage.
    2. Tap the menu icon and select Download or Save for Offline.

**Tip:** This is especially useful for reading articles or instructions when you won't have internet access, such as when traveling.

## 6. Managing Browser Tabs

The ability to open multiple tabs allows you to browse several websites at once. You can switch between tabs, close them, or open new ones as needed.

**Opening and Switching Tabs:**

1. **Open a New Tab:** In the browser, tap the plus (+) icon at the top to open a new tab.

2. **Switch Between Tabs:** To switch between tabs, tap the tabs icon (usually a square with a number in it) at the top of the screen. This will display all your open tabs. Tap a tab to switch to it.

3. **Close Tabs:** To close a tab, tap the X in the corner of the tab window, or swipe the tab away.

**Tip:** If you have too many tabs open, your browser might slow down. It's a good idea to periodically close tabs you no longer need.

---

### 7. Private Browsing Mode

If you want to browse the web without saving your history, cookies, or search queries, you can use Incognito Mode or Private Browsing.

**How to Open Incognito Mode:**

1. Open your browser.
2. Tap the menu icon (three dots).
3. Select New Incognito Tab or Private Tab.

When browsing in Incognito Mode, your activity isn't saved on the phone. However, your internet service provider can still track your browsing, so Incognito Mode is not completely anonymous.

**Tip:** Use Incognito Mode if you're on a shared device and don't want to leave traces of your browsing activity, such as when shopping for gifts or looking up sensitive information.

---

### 8. Keeping Your Browsing Safe

Browsing the internet on your Android phone is generally safe, but it's important to be aware of potential risks such as phishing scams, malware, and malicious websites.

**How to Stay Safe Online:**

- **Only Visit Secure Websites:** Look for "https" at the beginning of the website's address or a padlock icon. This means the site uses encryption to protect your data.
- **Avoid Suspicious Links:** Be cautious when clicking on links in emails, text messages, or unfamiliar websites. Scammers often use fake links to trick people into providing personal information.
- **Keep Your Browser Updated:** Regular updates to your browser help protect you from the latest security vulnerabilities. Your phone should automatically update the browser, but you can also check for updates manually in the Google Play Store.

**Tip:** Many browsers, including Google Chrome, have a built-in feature called Safe Browsing, which warns you if a website you're visiting is unsafe. Make sure this feature is turned on in your browser settings.

---

### 9. Clearing Your Browsing History

Over time, your browser will save a record of websites you've visited, as well as other data such as cookies and cached files. While this can speed up your browsing experience, you might want to clear this data occasionally for privacy or to free up space on your phone.

**How to Clear Your Browsing History:**

1. Open your browser and tap the menu icon.
2. Select History.
3. Tap Clear Browsing Data or Clear History.
4. Choose the time range (e.g., last hour, last day, or all time).
5. Select the data you want to clear (such as Browsing History, Cookies, and Cached Images).

6. Tap Clear Data.

**Tip:** Clearing your cache can also help fix issues like slow page loading or websites not displaying correctly.

---

## Conclusion

Browsing the internet on your Android phone opens up a world of information, entertainment, and communication at your fingertips. Whether you're reading the news, searching for information, or shopping online, understanding how to navigate websites, use tabs, and stay safe online will enhance your experience. With these tips, you're ready to explore the internet confidently and efficiently on your Android device.

---

# CHAPTER 9: DOWNLOADING APPS FROM THE GOOGLE PLAY STORE

One of the greatest advantages of having an Android phone is the vast selection of apps available through the Google Play Store. Whether you need tools for communication, entertainment, health, or daily tasks, there's an app for nearly every need. In this chapter, we'll walk you through the process of finding, downloading, and managing apps from the Play Store.

## 1. What is the Google Play Store?

The Google Play Store is the official app store for Android devices, where you can download apps, games, books, movies, and even music. It offers both free and paid apps, and it's the safest way to install apps on your device because all apps on the Play Store are checked for security and privacy concerns by Google.

Some apps are designed for fun, like games or music players, while others are practical, such as health trackers, navigation apps, and productivity tools. You can explore by category or search for something specific.

## 2. How to Access the Google Play Store

To start exploring apps, you'll need to access the Google Play Store on your Android phone. Here's how:

1. **Locate the Play Store App:** The Play Store app icon looks like a colourful triangle and should already be installed on your phone. You can find it on your home screen or in the app drawer (swipe up from the bottom of the screen

to open the app drawer).

2. **Sign in with Your Google Account:** To download apps, you'll need a Google account. If you don't have one, you'll be prompted to create one during your first visit to the Play Store.

3. **Open the Play Store:** Tap the Play Store icon to open it. You'll now see the home page, which displays recommended apps, games, and categories for you to explore.

---

### 3. Searching for Apps

Once you're inside the Play Store, you can either browse categories to discover apps or search for a specific app.

- **Search Bar:** At the top of the Play Store, you'll see a search bar. If you know the name of the app you want, simply type it in the search bar and press Enter. A list of relevant apps will appear, and you can tap on the app you're looking for.

**Example Search Terms:**

  - "WhatsApp" (for messaging)
  - "Spotify" (for music streaming)
  - "Google Maps" (for navigation)

- **Browse Categories:** If you're not sure what app you want, you can browse by categories like Entertainment, Health & Fitness, Education, Productivity, and Photography. Tap on a category to see popular and recommended apps in that section.

- **Editor's Choice and Top Charts:** These sections highlight some of the best and most popular apps, as selected by Google's editors and users.

---

### 4. How to Download and Install Apps

Once you've found the app you want, downloading it is a simple process. Follow these steps to install an app on your Android phone:

1. **Select the App:** Tap the app name to open its details page. This page will show you more information about the app, including screenshots, a description, user ratings, and reviews.

**Important Tip:** Before downloading, take a look at the app's rating and reviews. This can help you avoid poorly functioning or unsafe apps.

2. **Install the App:**
   - If the app is free, you'll see a green button labelled Install. Tap it to start the download process.
   - If the app has a price, the button will display the cost. You'll need to tap the price to purchase the app, and you'll be prompted to confirm your payment method. Once the purchase is complete, the app will begin downloading.

3. **Wait for Installation:** After tapping Install, the app will begin downloading and installing automatically. You can track its progress in the notification bar at the top of your screen.

4. **Open the App:** Once the app is installed, you'll see an Open button. Tap it to launch the app and start using it immediately. The app will also be added to your home screen or app drawer for future access.

---

## 5. Managing Your Installed Apps

Once you've downloaded several apps, it's important to know how to manage them effectively. You can organize, update, or even uninstall apps if they are no longer needed.

- **Viewing Installed Apps:** To view all the apps you've installed, open the Play Store, tap your profile icon (top-right corner), and select My apps & games. This will show you a list of all your installed apps.

- **Updating Apps:** Apps are regularly updated to fix bugs, add new features, or improve performance. To check for updates, go to My apps & games in the Play Store, and you'll see a list of apps with available updates. You can either update each one manually or tap Update All to update all apps at once.

- **Uninstalling Apps:** If you no longer need an app, uninstalling it will free up space on your phone. To uninstall an app:
    1. Go to Settings > Apps or find the app in the My apps & games section in the Play Store.
    2. Tap the app you want to remove.
    3. Select Uninstall. The app will be deleted from your phone.

## 6. In-App Purchases and Free vs. Paid Apps

While many apps are free to download, some apps offer additional features, content, or services through in-app purchases. These might include additional levels in a game, premium features in a productivity app, or removing ads from free apps.

- **Free Apps:** Many free apps are supported by ads. You can often upgrade to an ad-free version with an in-app purchase.

- **Paid Apps:** Some apps require a one-time purchase before downloading. Be sure to check the reviews and details before purchasing paid apps.

- **Subscriptions:** Some apps, like music streaming services or cloud storage, operate on a subscription model. These apps may offer a free trial period but will require payment after the trial ends.

**Tip:** Always monitor in-app purchases, especially if you share your phone with grandchildren or other family members. You can adjust your Google account settings to require password entry before making any purchases.

## 7. Ensuring App Security

One of the most important aspects of downloading apps is ensuring they are safe and secure. Follow these tips to protect your phone and personal data:

- **Download from Trusted Developers:** Stick to apps with good reviews, high download numbers, and well-known developers. Avoid unknown or poorly rated apps.

- **Check App Permissions:** When you install an app, it may ask for access to certain features on your phone, such as the camera, microphone, or contacts. Be cautious with apps that request excessive permissions, especially if those permissions don't make sense for the app's purpose (e.g., a flashlight app shouldn't need access to your contacts).

- **Enable Play Protect:** Google Play Protect scans apps for malware and harmful activity. To ensure it's enabled, open the Play Store, tap your profile icon, select Play Protect, and make sure it's turned on.

## Conclusion

The Google Play Store opens up a world of possibilities for your Android phone, allowing you to personalize your device, stay entertained, and make everyday tasks easier. Whether you're looking to improve your health, keep in touch with family, or just have fun, there's an app for nearly everything. With a few simple steps, you can search, download, and install apps that will enhance your phone's capabilities and make your life easier.

Don't hesitate to explore and try out new apps—you can always uninstall them if they don't meet your needs. With the power of the Google Play Store at your fingertips, you'll find endless ways to make the most of your Android smartphone.

# CHAPTER 10: ESSENTIAL APPS FOR SENIORS

Android phones offer a wide variety of apps designed to make everyday tasks simpler and more enjoyable for seniors. Whether you want to stay in touch with family, manage your health, or explore new hobbies, there are apps specifically built to meet your needs. This chapter will introduce you to easy-to-use apps that help you stay connected, organized, entertained, and safe. These apps are not only practical but also user-friendly, ensuring that even those who are less familiar with smartphones can benefit from them.

## 1. Communication Apps

Staying connected with family and friends is one of the most important uses of your Android phone. Thankfully, there are apps that make communicating easy, even if your loved ones are far away.

**WhatsApp:**

- **WhatsApp** is a free app for messaging, voice, and video calls. It's great for connecting with family members near and far without worrying about high phone bills, as it works over Wi-Fi or your phone's internet.
- **Why it's great for seniors:** WhatsApp is simple and reliable. You can send a quick text, make a phone call, or even see your family on a video call, all within the same

app.

**How to use it:**

1. **Install WhatsApp:** Go to the Google Play Store and search for WhatsApp.

2. **Sign up with your phone number**: Simply follow the steps to verify your phone number.

3. **Add contacts:** WhatsApp syncs with your contacts, so if your family is already using WhatsApp, you can easily message them.

**Facebook Messenger:**

- **Facebook Messenger** works alongside Facebook, allowing you to chat with your friends and family. You can use it for sending messages, photos, or even making video calls.

- **Why it's great for seniors:** If you already use Facebook to keep up with your family, Messenger lets you communicate with them directly without needing to switch apps.

**Tip:** Both apps allow you to make video calls, which can be a wonderful way to see loved ones when you can't be together in person.

---

## 2. Health and Wellness Apps

Staying healthy and keeping track of medications and fitness is a breeze with the right apps. There are several simple apps that can help you monitor your health, stay fit, and maintain a healthy lifestyle.

**Medisafe:**

- Medisafe is a medication reminder app that helps you keep track of when to take your pills. You can set up reminders for all your medications, so you never miss a dose.

- Why it's great for seniors: With an easy-to-use interface, Medisafe ensures that you get reminders to take your medicine on time, and it can even notify a loved one if you miss a dose.

**How to use it:**

1. Install Medisafe: Go to the Google Play Store and search for Medisafe.
2. Enter your medications: Input your prescription schedule, and Medisafe will send you timely reminders to help you stay on track.

**Google Fit:**

- Google Fit tracks your physical activity, such as steps, walking, and exercise. It's a simple way to make sure you're staying active, which is important for overall health.
- Why it's great for seniors: Google Fit is easy to use, even if you're just walking around the house or going for short walks. You can set goals for how much you want to move each day and monitor your progress.

**Tip:** If you have a fitness tracker like Fitbit, it can sync with Google Fit to help you keep track of all your activities in one place.

---

### 3. Entertainment and Learning Apps

In your downtime, you can use your Android phone for entertainment or to learn new things. Whether you enjoy music, books, or movies, these apps offer something for everyone.

**Spotify:**

- **Spotify** is a music app that allows you to listen to your favourite songs, artists, or even podcasts. It has playlists for every occasion, and you can explore music from different genres or time periods.
- **Why it's great for seniors:** Spotify's easy-to-navigate layout lets you find music you love, and you can create custom playlists to suit your mood.

**How to use it:**

1. **Install Spotify:** Download Spotify from the Google Play Store.
2. **Browse music:** You can search for specific artists or listen to curated playlists for everything from relaxing music to oldies.

### YouTube:

- **YouTube** is a video app where you can watch just about anything, from cooking shows and travel vlogs to how-to tutorials. You can even listen to music or watch concerts.
- **Why it's great for seniors:** YouTube makes it easy to find videos on your favourite topics. Whether you want to watch a cooking tutorial or a movie review, YouTube has it.

### How to use it:

1. Open YouTube: The app is often pre-installed on most Android phones.
2. Search for content: Type in what you'd like to watch, such as "classic movies," "exercise for seniors," or "cooking tips," and enjoy!

### Audible:

- **Audible** is an audiobook app that lets you listen to books instead of reading them. It's perfect for when you want to relax and enjoy a good story without straining your eyes.
- **Why it's great for seniors:** Audible's audiobooks are a great way to enjoy literature, especially if you have trouble reading for long periods. You can choose from thousands of titles.

### 4. Finance and Budgeting Apps

Managing finances can be simplified with apps designed to help you track your spending, pay bills, and budget more easily.

### Mint:

- **Mint** helps you keep track of your expenses, set budgets, and even monitor your accounts. You can link your bank accounts and credit cards to see all your financial information in one place.

- **Why it's great for seniors:** Mint is easy to navigate, with simple charts and graphs to help you understand where your money is going and how to stick to a budget.

**Tip:** Set up alerts on these apps to notify you of any unusual activity or when a payment is due, so you can stay on top of your finances effortlessly.

## 5. Safety and Emergency Apps

There are also several apps designed to help keep you safe and connected to emergency services or family members in case of a problem.

**Life360:**

- **Life360** is a family locator app that allows your loved ones to check in on you and see your location in real-time. It's especially helpful if you're out and about and want someone to know where you are.
- **Why it's great for seniors:** Life360 gives you peace of mind, allowing family members to track your location if necessary. It also has a panic button feature to alert family in case of an emergency.

**How to use it:**

1. Download Life360: Get the app from the Google Play Store.
2. Invite family members: You can add trusted family members to your network, so they can see where you are.

**Red Panic Button:**

- **Red Panic Button** is an emergency app that lets you alert your family or friends with the press of a button. It sends them your location and a distress message, making it easy to get help when needed.
- **Why it's great for seniors:** This app can be a lifesaver if

you need help quickly. The one-button interface is simple and easy to use.

**Tip:** Emergency apps like these are helpful if you ever find yourself needing assistance quickly, especially if you live alone or are prone to falls.

---

## Conclusion

These essential apps are designed to simplify your life and keep you connected, entertained, and safe. Whether you're managing your health, staying in touch with family, or enjoying some entertainment, your Android phone can make these tasks easier and more enjoyable. As you continue exploring your phone's capabilities, you'll find that these apps help you get the most out of your Android experience.

---

# CHAPTER 11: MANAGING NOTIFICATIONS AND ALERTS

Your Android phone keeps you informed about everything from incoming messages and calls to updates from apps and important system notifications. While these notifications are helpful, they can sometimes become overwhelming. Learning how to manage notifications and alerts can help you stay organized, reduce distractions, and ensure you only receive the notifications that are most important to you. In this chapter, we'll explore how to customize, prioritize, and control notifications, as well as how to mute or block alerts when needed.

## 1. Understanding Notifications on Android

Notifications are alerts from apps or your phone system that appear in the status bar at the top of your screen. They are designed to notify you of important events, like receiving a text message, an upcoming calendar event, or a new email. Notifications can appear as banners, sounds, or vibrations depending on your preferences and settings.

**Types of Notifications:**

- **App Notifications:** Alerts from apps like messaging apps, email clients, social media apps, and news apps. For example, a text message notification from WhatsApp or an email notification from Gmail.

- **System Notifications:** These come from your phone's system, such as updates, battery alerts, or storage space warnings.
- **Silent Notifications:** These notifications appear in your status bar but do not make a sound or vibration. Examples include background tasks or app updates.

## 2. Viewing and Interacting with Notifications

When a notification appears, you can interact with it directly from the Notification Shade. The Notification Shade is the area that appears when you swipe down from the top of the screen.

### How to View Notifications:

1. **Swipe Down:** To see all of your notifications, swipe down from the top of the screen to open the Notification Shade. Here you will see a list of recent notifications, each accompanied by the app's icon and a brief description of the alert.
2. **Tap to Open:** If you want to interact with a notification (e.g., to reply to a message or view a calendar reminder), tap on the notification to open the relevant app.

### Managing Notifications:

- **Dismiss a Notification:** If you don't want to deal with a notification right away, you can dismiss it by swiping it to the left or right.
- **Expand a Notification:** Some notifications, such as emails or messages, offer more options when expanded. To expand, tap the small arrow next to the notification or use two fingers to swipe down on the notification.
- **Snooze a Notification:** If you don't want to deal with a notification now but want a reminder later, swipe the notification slightly left or right and tap the snooze icon (a clock). You can choose how long to snooze the notification.

**Tip:** If you frequently miss notifications, make sure the Do Not Disturb mode isn't enabled or review your notification settings to ensure important alerts are allowed.

---

### 3. Customizing Notification Settings

Android gives you full control over how notifications behave for each app on your phone. You can adjust whether an app sends notifications, how notifications are displayed, and what types of alerts you receive (e.g., sound, vibration, or silent).

**How to Customize Notification Settings:**

1. **Open Settings:** Swipe down from the top of the screen and tap the gear icon to open Settings.

2. **Go to Notifications:** Scroll down and tap Apps & Notifications or simply Notifications, depending on your phone model.

3. **Select an App:** You'll see a list of apps that have sent notifications recently. Tap an app to adjust its notification settings.

4. **Customize Notification Options:**

   ◦ **Allow or Block Notifications**: Toggle the switch to turn notifications for that app on or off entirely.

   ◦ **Sound and Vibration: Choose whether notifications from the app should make a sound, vibrate, or stay silent.**

   ◦ **Lock Screen: Decide whether notifications should appear on the lock screen or only after you unlock the phone.**

   ◦ **Priority: For apps you want to prioritize, you can set notifications to appear at the top of the Notification Shade or trigger more noticeable alerts, like flashing lights or a higher-volume sound.**

**Tip:** If an app is sending too many notifications but you don't want to block them completely, try switching to Silent Notifications to reduce the noise while still receiving updates.

## 4. Managing Persistent Notifications

Some apps and services, such as weather apps or system processes, send persistent notifications that stay at the top of the Notification Shade until you address them. While these notifications can be useful, they can also clutter your screen if you don't need them constantly.

### How to Handle Persistent Notifications:

1. **Press and Hold:** When you receive a persistent notification, press and hold it to bring up options.
2. **Change Settings:** Tap Notification Settings to adjust how persistent notifications are displayed. You can choose to keep them in the Notification Shade but silence them, or you can turn them off entirely.
3. **Hide Certain Notifications:** If you want to continue receiving notifications but don't want to see the icon in the status bar, you can choose to hide it while keeping the alert silent.

**Tip:** For apps like email or messaging, which you need notifications for but don't want constant alerts, consider changing them to silent but visible notifications.

## 5. Do Not Disturb Mode

If you need some quiet time without being disturbed by notifications, calls, or alerts, you can use Do Not Disturb mode. This feature allows you to block all or specific notifications for a period of time, making it perfect for when you're sleeping, in a meeting, or just need a break.

### How to Enable Do Not Disturb Mode:

1. **Quick Access:** Swipe down from the top of the screen to open the Quick Settings panel. Look for the Do Not Disturb icon (a circle with a line through it) and tap it.

## 2. Customize Settings:

- ○ **Allow Exceptions:** In Settings > Sound > Do Not Disturb, you can specify exceptions. For example, you might allow calls from certain contacts or allow alarms to ring even when Do Not Disturb is on.
- ○ **Schedules: You can schedule Do Not Disturb to turn on automatically at certain times, such as overnight or during work hours.**

**Tip:** You can customize Do Not Disturb to still allow priority contacts (like family members) to get through in case of emergencies.

## 6. Managing Notification Channels

Android offers fine-grained control over notifications through notification channels. Each app can send different types of notifications (e.g., for different tasks or updates), and you can control each one individually.

**How to Manage Notification Channels:**

1. **Open Notification Settings:** Go to Settings > Apps & Notifications > See All Apps.
2. **Select an App:** Choose the app you want to customize notifications for.
3. **Manage Channels:** If the app supports multiple notification channels, you'll see a list of different types of notifications (e.g., "Message notifications," "Group chat notifications"). You can enable or disable specific channels or customize how notifications for that channel behave (sound, vibration, silent, etc.).

**Example:** In a messaging app, you might want to allow notifications for individual chats but disable notifications for group chats to avoid being overwhelmed.

**Tip:** Use notification channels to control which notifications you care about within an app, rather than turning all notifications on or off.

---

## 7. Controlling App Badge Notifications

App icon badges are the small dots or numbers that appear on an app's icon on the home screen to let you know there are new notifications. Some people find these helpful, while others find them distracting.

**How to Enable or Disable App Badges:**

1. **Go to Settings:** Open Settings > Apps & Notifications > Notifications.
2. App Icon Badges: Scroll down to find the App Icon Badges option and toggle it on or off.
3. **Customize Badges:** Some Android phones let you control which apps display badges. You can set badges to show a simple dot or a number indicating how many new notifications are available.

**Tip:** App badges can be helpful for seeing at a glance which apps have new notifications without needing to open the app.

---

## 8. Muting or Blocking Specific Notifications

If an app is sending too many notifications, you can either mute or block it completely. This can be helpful for apps that send non-urgent updates, promotional notifications, or persistent alerts that you don't need to see regularly.

**How to Mute or Block Notifications:**

1. **Open Notification Settings:** Go to Settings > Apps & Notifications > See All Apps.
2. **Choose the App:** Select the app you want to block notifications for.
3. **Disable Notifications:** Toggle off the option for Allow Notifications to block notifications entirely, or customize the notification behaviour to reduce the number of alerts.

**Tip:** Muting or blocking non-essential notifications can help you focus on important notifications without being distracted by less urgent ones.

## Conclusion

Managing notifications on your Android phone is key to staying organized and avoiding distractions. By customizing how different apps and alerts behave, you can ensure that you're only notified about the things that matter most to you. Whether it's silencing less important alerts, using Do Not Disturb mode to block all notifications temporarily, or using notification channels to control different types of notifications within the same app, you now have the tools to make your phone's alerts work for you

# CHAPTER 12: CUSTOMIZING YOUR PHONE

One of the most enjoyable features of Android phones is the ability to personalize and customize nearly every aspect of the device to suit your individual style and preferences. Whether you want to change the look of your home screen, adjust sounds and ringtones, or even install a custom launcher, Android gives you the freedom to make your phone uniquely yours. In this chapter, we'll explore the different ways you can customize your phone, making it an extension of your personality and needs.

## 1. Changing Your Wallpaper

The first and easiest way to personalize your phone is by changing the wallpaper, the background image that appears on your home screen and lock screen. You can choose from pre-installed wallpapers, use a photo from your gallery, or download wallpaper apps for even more options.

**How to Change Your Wallpaper:**

1. **Press and Hold the Home Screen:** On your home screen, press and hold an empty area until a menu appears.

2. **Select Wallpapers:** Tap on Wallpapers or Wallpaper & Style from the menu.

3. **Choose a Wallpaper Source:**

   ◦ **Built-in Wallpapers**: Browse through the phone's default wallpapers by selecting

Wallpapers or My Photos.

- ◦ **Gallery: If you want to use one of your own photos, tap Gallery and select an image.**
- ◦ **Live Wallpapers: Some Android phones offer animated or "live" wallpapers that move on your screen.**

4. **Set the Wallpaper:** Once you've chosen your wallpaper, tap Set Wallpaper. You can choose to apply it to the home screen, lock screen, or both.

**Tip:** Simple, uncluttered wallpapers can make your app icons easier to see. You can change your wallpaper as often as you like, so feel free to experiment!

## 2. Rearranging and Organizing Apps on Your Home Screen

Your home screen is where you access your most frequently used apps, so it's important to keep it organized. Android allows you to move, remove, and group apps as you see fit.

**Rearranging Apps:**

- **Move an App:** Press and hold an app icon until it "floats." You can then drag it to a different position on the screen. Release it when it's in the desired spot.
- **Create App Folders:** If you want to group similar apps together (like social media or productivity apps), drag one app icon onto another to create a folder. You can then name the folder (e.g., "Games" or "Work").
- **Add Apps to the Home Screen:** To add an app that's not on your home screen, swipe up to open the App Drawer. Find the app, then press and hold the icon and drag it to the home screen.

**Tip:** Consider keeping your most-used apps within easy reach on the dock (the area at the bottom of the home screen). This way, they're always accessible, no matter which home screen page you're on.

### 3. Widgets: Quick Access to Information

Widgets are interactive elements that sit on your home screen and give you quick access to information or controls without opening an app. For example, you can add a weather widget that displays the current temperature, or a calendar widget that shows upcoming events.

**How to Add a Widget:**

1. **Long-press on the Home Screen:** Press and hold an empty area on your home screen until the customization menu appears.
2. **Tap Widgets:** In the menu that appears, tap Widgets.
3. **Choose a Widget:** Browse through the available widgets, which are often organized by app. For example, you'll find widgets for Calendar, Weather, Clock, and more.
4. **Place the Widget:** Press and hold the widget you want, then drag it to the home screen. You can adjust its size by pressing and holding it, then dragging the edges.

**Tip:** Some widgets, like music controls or to-do lists, can save you time by providing quick access to app functions directly from the home screen.

### 4. Changing Your Ringtone and Notification Sounds

Personalizing your phone's ringtones and notification sounds is a fun way to make your phone feel more like yours. You can choose from built-in sounds or use custom sounds like songs or audio clips.

**How to Change Ringtone and Notification Sounds:**

1. **Open Settings:** Swipe down from the top of the screen and tap the Settings icon (a gear).
2. **Tap Sound or Sound & Vibration**: In the settings menu, look for Sound or Sound & Vibration, depending on your phone model.
3. **Change Ringtone:** Tap Phone Ringtone to see a list of

available ringtones. Tap on a ringtone to hear a preview, then tap OK to set it.

4. **Change Notification Sound:** To change the sound for notifications like messages or app alerts, tap Notification Sound and choose from the list of available options.

5. **Custom Ringtones and Sounds:** If you want to use a custom sound, tap Add Ringtone or Add Notification Sound. You can select audio files from your music library or download new ringtones from apps like Zedge.

**Tip:** Assign custom ringtones to specific contacts. This way, you'll know who's calling just by the sound of the ringtone!

## 5. Customizing the Lock Screen

Your lock screen is what you see before you unlock your phone. You can customize it to show the information you want, such as the time, date, notifications, and shortcuts to certain apps.

**How to Customize the Lock Screen:**

1. **Go to Settings:** Open Settings and tap Lock Screen or Lock Screen Settings.

2. **Change Shortcuts:** Many Android phones allow you to place shortcuts to apps (such as the Camera or Messages) on the lock screen. Tap Shortcuts and choose the apps you want to access without unlocking your phone.

3. **Display Notifications:** You can control whether notifications appear on your lock screen. Tap Notifications on Lock Screen and choose whether to show all notifications, hide sensitive information, or hide notifications altogether.

**Tip:** If you prefer privacy, consider hiding detailed notifications on the lock screen, so only the app's name appears without revealing the full message.

## 6. Customizing the Keyboard

The keyboard is one of the most frequently used tools on your phone, and Android lets you personalize it in several ways, including changing its look, adding languages, or adjusting settings to make typing more comfortable.

**How to Customize the Keyboard:**

1. **Open Settings:** Go to Settings > System > Languages & Input.

2. **Select Virtual Keyboard:** Tap Virtual Keyboard to see the available keyboards on your phone.

3. **Customize Your Keyboard:**
   - **Theme:** Some keyboards, such as Gboard (Google's keyboard), allow you to change the keyboard's appearance. Go to the Gboard settings, tap Theme, and select from light, dark, or custom backgrounds.
   - **Typing Preferences: Adjust the size of the keys, enable or disable auto-correction, and turn on vibration or sound feedback when typing.**
   - **Add Languages: If you type in multiple languages, you can add additional language keyboards in the Languages section.**

**Tip:** If you want more keyboard customization options, consider downloading third-party keyboards like SwiftKey or Fleksy, which offer even more themes and features.

---

### 7. Installing and Using Custom Launchers

A launcher is the interface that controls the home screen, app drawer, and how you interact with the system. Android allows you to install custom launchers, which can dramatically change the look and feel of your phone. Popular launchers like Nova Launcher, Microsoft Launcher, and Action Launcher offer extra customization options.

**How to Install and Use a Custom Launcher:**

1. **Download a Launcher:** Go to the Google Play Store

and search for custom launchers (e.g., Nova Launcher). Download and install the launcher you want.

2. **Set the Launcher as Default:** After installing, open the launcher, and your phone will ask if you want to set it as the default home app. Select Yes to switch.

3. **Customize the Launcher:** Launchers allow you to tweak almost every aspect of your phone, from icon shapes to animations. Explore the settings of your chosen launcher to adjust the layout, change transition animations, and apply themes or icon packs.

**Tip:** Launchers can make your phone feel completely new. Experiment with different launchers until you find the one that fits your style and preferences.

## 8. Using Themes and Icon Packs

Many Android phones, particularly Samsung and Xiaomi models, allow you to apply themes that change the overall appearance of your phone. These themes can modify wallpapers, icons, fonts, and even the colours of the system interface.

**How to Apply a Theme:**

1. **Open Settings:** Go to Settings > Themes or Wallpaper & Themes, depending on your phone model.

2. **Browse Themes:** You'll find a selection of free and paid themes. Browse the available options and tap on one to see a preview.

3. **Download and Apply:** Tap Download to install the theme, then select Apply to activate it on your phone.

**How to Use Icon Packs:**

1. **Download an Icon Pack:** Icon packs change the appearance of your app icons. You can download icon packs from the Google Play Store (e.g., Whicons, CandyCons).

2. **Apply Icon Pack:** Depending on your launcher or phone,

you may need a custom launcher to apply icon packs. Open the launcher's settings and look for the Icon Pack option, then select the one you downloaded.

**Tip:** Changing your icons and theme can give your phone a whole new aesthetic. You can mix and match themes and icon packs for a unique look.

## 9. Adjusting Display Settings

Customizing your phone's display settings can improve your viewing experience, especially if you have specific preferences regarding brightness, font size, and colour balance.

**How to Customize Display Settings:**

1. **Brightness:** Go to Settings > Display and adjust the brightness slider. You can also enable Adaptive Brightness, which automatically adjusts the screen brightness based on your surroundings.

2. **Font Size and Display Size:** If the text on your phone is too small, you can increase the Font Size or Display Size by going to Settings > Display and selecting Font Size or Display Size.

3. **Dark Mode:** Dark Mode changes the background of menus and some apps to a dark colour, which can reduce eye strain in low-light environments. Enable Dark Mode by going to Settings > Display and turning on Dark Mode or Night Mode.

**Tip:** Adjusting display settings can make your phone easier to use, especially if you have difficulty reading small text or if your phone's screen feels too bright.

## Conclusion

Customizing your Android phone is not only fun but also practical. By tailoring the look and feel of your device, you can create a personalized experience that's more enjoyable and easier to use. From changing wallpapers and ringtones to adjusting display settings and using custom launchers, you have endless possibilities to make your phone reflect your personality and preferences. Explore the options available and make your phone truly your own.

# CHAPTER 13: BATTERY LIFE TIPS AND TRICKS

Battery life is a critical concern for most smartphone users, especially as we rely on our phones for everything from communication to entertainment and productivity. Android phones come with several built-in tools and settings that allow you to monitor and improve battery life. In this chapter, we'll explore a range of tips, tricks, and strategies to help you extend your phone's battery life, troubleshoot battery drain issues, and make sure your phone lasts longer between charges.

## 1. Understanding Your Battery Usage

The first step in managing your battery life is understanding how your phone is using power. Android phones provide detailed information about which apps and services are consuming the most battery.

**How to View Battery Usage:**

1. **Open Settings:** Swipe down from the top of the screen and tap the Settings icon (a gear).
2. **Tap Battery:** Scroll down and select Battery or Battery Usage. Here, you'll see an overview of your current battery level and estimated time remaining.
3. **Check App Usage:** Tap Battery Usage to see a list of apps and services that have used battery power in the last few hours or days. Apps that consume a lot of power will be listed at the top.

**Tip:** If you notice an app using an unusual amount of battery, consider closing it, updating it, or limiting its background activity.

## 2. Reducing Screen Brightness and Display Time

Your phone's screen is one of the biggest battery drainers, especially if it's set to a high brightness level. Reducing the screen's brightness and turning it off when not in use are two simple ways to extend battery life.

**Lowering Screen Brightness:**

1. **Open Settings:** Go to Settings > Display.
2. **Adjust Brightness:** Drag the brightness slider to the left to lower the brightness. You can also access this slider by swiping down from the top of the screen to open the Quick Settings panel.
3. **Enable Adaptive Brightness:** If you want your phone to automatically adjust brightness based on the surrounding light, enable Adaptive Brightness in the Display settings. This feature dims the screen in darker environments to conserve battery.

**Tip:** Keeping the brightness around 50% or lower can significantly improve battery life.

**Reduce Screen Timeout:**

- The Screen Timeout setting controls how long the screen stays on after inactivity. The shorter the timeout, the less battery is consumed.
    1. Go to Settings > Display.
    2. Tap Screen Timeout and select a shorter interval (e.g., 30 seconds or 1 minute).

## 3. Managing Background Apps and Processes

Even when you're not actively using them, many apps continue running in the background, consuming battery power for updates, notifications, and other processes. Limiting background activity can reduce battery drain significantly.

**How to Limit Background Activity:**

1. Open Settings: Go to Settings > Battery.
2. Battery Saver: Tap Battery Saver and turn it on. This feature limits background activity, such as updates and syncing, to conserve battery.
3. Restrict Background Activity for Specific Apps:
   - Go to Settings > Apps & Notifications.
   - Select an app, tap Battery, and choose Restrict Background Activity. This prevents the app from running in the background when not in use.

**Tip:** Apps like social media, email, and messaging services often run in the background. If you don't need constant updates, restrict their background activity to save power.

---

### 4. Using Battery Saver Mode

Most Android phones come with a Battery Saver mode, which automatically reduces power consumption by limiting certain features and background processes.

**How to Enable Battery Saver Mode:**

1. **Quick Settings:** Swipe down from the top of the screen to open the Quick Settings panel and tap the Battery Saver icon (it looks like a battery with a plus sign).
2. **Manual Settings:** You can also enable it manually by going to Settings > Battery > Battery Saver and toggling it on.

**How Battery Saver Works:**

- Limits background processes, syncing, and location services.
- Reduces screen brightness and disables visual effects like animations.
- Disables features like always-on display or background app refresh.

**Tip:** You can set Battery Saver mode to automatically turn on when your battery reaches a certain percentage, such as 15% or 20%, to extend the remaining battery life.

---

### 5. Turning Off Unused Connectivity Features

Leaving features like Wi-Fi, Bluetooth, Location Services, and NFC on when not in use can quickly drain your battery. Managing these features can help conserve power throughout the day.

**How to Manage Connectivity Features:**

1. **Wi-Fi:** Turn off Wi-Fi when you're not connected to a network. Swipe down to open Quick Settings and tap the Wi-Fi icon to disable it.

2. **Bluetooth:** Turn off Bluetooth when you're not using wireless devices like headphones. Tap the Bluetooth icon in the Quick Settings to disable it.

3. **Location Services (GPS):** Location services use a lot of battery, especially for apps like Google Maps. Go to Settings > Location and toggle it off when you're not using it.

4. **NFC (Near Field Communication):** If you don't use NFC (often used for mobile payments), disable it in Settings > Connections > NFC.

**Tip:** For convenience, you can leave Wi-Fi on but disable automatic scanning for networks when it's not connected by going to Settings > Wi-Fi > Advanced > Scanning Always Available.

---

### 6. Optimizing Apps for Better Battery Performance

Android allows you to optimize apps for better battery performance, which limits unnecessary battery usage without affecting how the app functions when you're actively using it.

**How to Optimize Apps:**

1. **Open Settings:** Go to Settings > Battery.

2. **Battery Optimization:** Tap Battery Optimization or Optimize Battery Usage.

3. **Select Apps to Optimize:** You'll see a list of apps with their optimization settings. Apps that are optimized will use less battery when running in the background. Ensure that power-hungry apps are optimized.

**Tip:** Most apps are set to optimize automatically, but if an app is draining your battery unnecessarily, you can manually enable optimization.

## 7. Minimizing Use of Battery-Intensive Apps

Certain apps and features, such as games, streaming video, and navigation apps, are more battery-intensive than others. Identifying which apps are consuming the most power can help you manage their usage.

**How to Identify Power-Hungry Apps:**

1. **Open Settings:** Go to Settings > Battery.
2. **View Battery Usage:** Tap Battery Usage to see a list of apps and services that are using your battery.
3. **Manage Heavy Users:** Apps like YouTube, Google Maps, or high-performance games may consume a significant amount of battery. Limit your use of these apps when you're trying to conserve battery.

**Tip:** Instead of watching long videos on mobile data, download them when you're on Wi-Fi. Likewise, using offline navigation apps can save battery when traveling.

## 8. Controlling Notifications and Alerts

Frequent notifications and alerts from apps can drain your battery, especially if they include sound, vibrations, or pop-up banners. Customizing your notification settings can help extend battery life.

**How to Control Notifications:**

1. **Open Settings:** Go to Settings > Notifications or Apps & Notifications.
2. **Select an App:** Choose the apps that send you the most

notifications.

3. **Customize Notifications:**
   - **Disable Unnecessary Notifications:** If you don't need frequent updates from an app, turn off its notifications.
   - **Silent Notifications:** You can set notifications to silent so that they don't trigger sounds or vibrations, which consume battery.

**Tip:** Reducing the number of notifications for less important apps can help save battery and reduce distractions.

---

## 9. Using Dark Mode

Dark Mode is a feature that changes the background of apps and the system interface to dark colours, which reduces battery usage on phones with OLED or AMOLED screens. Since dark pixels use less power than bright ones, Dark Mode can extend battery life when used consistently.

**How to Enable Dark Mode:**

1. **Open Settings:** Go to Settings > Display.
2. **Enable Dark Mode:** Toggle Dark Mode or Night Mode on. This will apply the dark theme to the system interface and compatible apps.

**Tip:** You can set Dark Mode to turn on automatically at certain times, like sunset, or leave it on permanently to save battery throughout the day.

---

## 10. Updating Your Phone's Software

Manufacturers regularly release software updates that improve battery performance by fixing bugs, optimizing apps, and improving system efficiency. Keeping your phone's software up to date is essential for ensuring the best battery life.

**How to Check for Updates:**

1. **Open Settings:** Go to Settings > Software Update or System > System Update.

2. **Check for Updates:** Tap Check for Updates and follow the instructions to install any available updates.

**Tip:** It's a good idea to enable automatic updates to ensure your phone is always running the latest, most optimized software.

## 11. Managing Battery Health for Long-Term Use

Over time, your phone's battery may degrade, reducing its capacity and performance. While this is a natural process for lithium-ion batteries, there are steps you can take to maintain battery health for longer.

**Tips for Preserving Battery Health:**

- **Avoid Extreme Temperatures:** Keep your phone out of extreme heat or cold, as both can degrade battery life. Avoid leaving your phone in direct sunlight or a hot car.
- **Charge Smartly:** Try not to let your battery drop below 20% or charge it to 100% all the time. Ideally, keep it between 20% and 80% to extend battery life.
- **Use Original Chargers:** Using third-party or incompatible chargers can damage your battery over time. Stick to the charger provided by the manufacturer or use a high-quality replacement.

## Conclusion

Maximizing your Android phone's battery life is about managing the balance between performance and power consumption. With careful adjustments to your settings—such as lowering screen brightness, limiting background activity, and using Battery Saver mode—you can ensure your phone lasts longer between charges. By following these tips and tricks, you'll be better equipped to manage your battery life efficiently, whether you're at home, at work, or on the go

# CHAPTER 14: STAYING SAFE: SECURITY AND PRIVACY

Your Android phone contains a lot of personal information, from contact lists and emails to photos, financial data, and apps that may store sensitive data. Keeping your phone secure and maintaining your privacy is essential in today's world, where cyber threats and data breaches are increasingly common. In this chapter, we'll explore the best practices for securing your phone, managing privacy settings, and protecting your personal information from unauthorized access.

---

**1. Securing Your Phone with Lock Screen Protection**

The first line of defence for your phone's security is setting up a lock screen that requires a PIN, password, pattern, or biometric authentication (such as fingerprint or facial recognition). This ensures that if your phone is lost or stolen, unauthorized users cannot access your personal data.

**How to Set Up Lock Screen Security:**

1. **Open Settings:** Go to Settings > Security or Lock Screen & Security, depending on your phone model.
2. **Select Screen Lock Type**: Tap Screen Lock and choose from one of the following options:
    - PIN: A 4- or 6-digit numerical code.
    - Password: A combination of letters, numbers, and symbols.

- ◦ Pattern: A swipe pattern you create by connecting dots.
- ◦ Fingerprint or Face Recognition: Biometric security options available on most modern Android devices.

3. **Confirm Your Choice**: Once you've chosen a screen lock method, follow the on-screen prompts to set it up.

**Tip:** Biometric security (fingerprint or facial recognition) is often faster and more convenient, but it's always a good idea to have a backup PIN or password in case biometric methods fail.

## 2. Using Two-Factor Authentication (2FA)

Two-Factor Authentication (2FA) adds an extra layer of security to your accounts by requiring two forms of verification—typically something you know (like a password) and something you have (like a phone or a security code). It's one of the most effective ways to protect your online accounts from unauthorized access.

**How to Enable 2FA:**

1. **Open the Account Settings:** For most online services (like Google, Facebook, or your banking app), go to your account settings on their website or app.

2. **Find the Security Section:** Look for the Security or Two-Factor Authentication option.

3. **Set Up 2FA:** Follow the instructions to enable 2FA. You may be asked to link your phone number or use an authentication app (like Google Authenticator or Authy) to generate security codes.

4. **Verify Your Identity:** Once 2FA is set up, you'll be required to enter a verification code sent to your phone whenever you log in from a new device.

**Tip:** Many apps also offer the option to use backup codes—keep these in a secure location in case you lose access to your phone.

## 3. Keeping Your Phone Updated

Regular software updates are essential for security because they include important security patches that protect your phone from the latest vulnerabilities. Android updates also improve system stability and performance, making your phone more efficient.

**How to Check for Updates:**

1. **Open Settings:** Go to Settings > System > Software Update or System Update.
2. **Check for Updates:** Tap Check for Updates to see if a new version of Android or a security patch is available.
3. **Install Updates:** If an update is available, follow the instructions to download and install it. Your phone may restart during this process.

**Tip:** Enabling automatic updates ensures that your phone is always protected with the latest security patches.

---

**4. Managing App Permissions**

Apps often request access to features or data on your phone (like your location, contacts, or camera), but not all apps need the permissions they ask for. Controlling which permissions apps have helps protect your privacy and limits the data apps can access.

**How to Manage App Permissions:**

1. **Open Settings:** Go to Settings > Apps or Apps & Notifications.
2. **Select an App:** Choose the app whose permissions you want to review.
3. **Tap Permissions:** Tap Permissions to see what access the app has (e.g., location, contacts, microphone).
4. **Enable or Disable Permissions:** Toggle permissions on or off depending on what you're comfortable allowing. For example, if a photo-editing app asks for access to your location, you can deny it unless it's necessary.

**Tip:** Be cautious of apps that request unnecessary or excessive permissions, especially if they ask for access to sensitive features like your contacts, messages, or camera without a clear reason.

## 5. Using Find My Device for Lost or Stolen Phones

Losing your phone can be a frustrating experience, but Android has built-in tools to help you locate, lock, or erase your device remotely. The Find My Device feature allows you to track your phone in real time and secure it if it's lost or stolen.

### How to Enable Find My Device:

1. **Open Settings:** Go to Settings > Security.
2. **Find My Device:** Tap Find My Device and make sure it's toggled on.
3. **Track Your Device:** If you lose your phone, visit the Find My Device website (findmydevice.google.com) from a computer or another phone. Log in with your Google account to track your device's location.

### Options for Lost Devices:

- **Ring Your Phone**: Make your phone ring at full volume, even if it's on silent, to help you locate it.
- **Lock Your Phone:** Remotely lock your phone and display a message or phone number for someone to contact you if they find it.
- **Erase Your Phone:** As a last resort, you can erase all the data on your phone to prevent anyone from accessing your information.

**Tip:** Make sure Location Services is turned on for Find My Device to work effectively.

## 6. Avoiding Phishing and Scams

Phishing scams are attempts by cybercriminals to trick you into revealing personal information (like passwords or credit card details) through fraudulent emails, text messages, or websites. Being able to recognize and avoid phishing attempts is crucial for staying safe online.

**How to Identify Phishing Scams:**

- **Unsolicited Messages:** Be wary of unsolicited emails or text messages that ask for personal information, especially if they claim to be from your bank, a government agency, or a well-known company.
- **Suspicious Links:** Never click on links in emails or texts unless you're sure they're legitimate. Phishing links often look similar to real websites but are slightly altered (e.g., "g00gle.com" instead of "google.com").
- **Requests for Personal Information:** Legitimate companies will never ask for your password or financial information via email or text.

**What to Do if You Suspect Phishing:**

1. **Delete the Message:** If you receive a suspicious email or text, delete it immediately without clicking any links.
2. **Report the Scam:** Many email providers allow you to report phishing messages. For example, in Gmail, open the email, click the three-dot menu, and select Report Phishing.

**Tip:** Use a spam filter in your email app to block most phishing attempts before they reach your inbox.

---

### 7. Installing Trusted Apps Only

Downloading apps from trusted sources is essential for avoiding malware, viruses, and spyware. Android's Google Play Store is the safest place to download apps because Google screens apps for security. However, installing apps from unknown or third-party sources can expose your phone to risks.

**How to Install Trusted Apps:**

1. **Use the Google Play Store:** Always download apps from the Google Play Store, were Google reviews apps for security.
2. **Check App Reviews and Ratings:** Before downloading an app, check its user reviews and ratings. Poor reviews or

complaints about security or excessive ads may be red flags.

3. **Avoid Third-Party App Stores:** Avoid downloading apps from third-party app stores or websites unless you trust the source.

**Tip:** If you must install an app from an external source (like a business or trusted developer), go to Settings > Security > Install Unknown Apps and enable it only for that specific app, then disable it again after installation.

## 8. Using a VPN for Private Browsing

If you're concerned about your privacy when browsing the internet, using a VPN (Virtual Private Network) can help protect your personal information. A VPN encrypts your internet connection, making it harder for hackers, advertisers, or even your internet provider to track your online activities.

**How to Use a VPN on Android:**

1. **Download a VPN App:** Go to the Google Play Store and search for a reputable VPN app, such as ExpressVPN, NordVPN, or TunnelBear.

2. **Install and Open the App:** Once installed, open the VPN app and follow the setup instructions.

3. **Turn on the VPN:** Once connected, your internet traffic will be encrypted, making it more difficult for third parties to access your data.

**Tip:** Using a VPN is particularly useful when browsing on public Wi-Fi networks, such as in cafes, airports, or hotels, as these networks are often less secure.

## 9. Encrypting Your Data

Android devices come with the option to encrypt your phone, which means that all the data on your device is stored in a scrambled, unreadable format. Encryption makes it much more difficult for someone to access your data if your phone is lost or stolen.

**How to Enable Encryption:**

1. **Open Settings:** Go to Settings > Security or Security & Privacy.

2. **Encrypt Device:** Tap Encrypt Phone or Encrypt Data, then follow the on-screen instructions. You may need to connect your phone to a charger during the encryption process.

3. **Confirm Lock Screen:** Encryption works in conjunction with your lock screen security (PIN, password, or biometric lock), so make sure you have a secure lock screen in place.

**Tip:** Encryption may slow down older devices slightly, but it provides an added layer of protection for sensitive data.

---

**10. Securing Your Google Account**

Your Google account is the key to many services on your Android phone, including Gmail, Google Drive, Google Photos, and the Play Store. Securing this account is crucial for protecting your data across all Google services.

**How to Secure Your Google Account:**

1. **Enable 2-Step Verification:** Go to myaccount.google.com and enable 2-Step Verification (also known as two-factor authentication) for your Google account. This requires both your password and a security code sent to your phone to log in.

2. **Review Account Activity:** Regularly check your Google Account Activity to see if any unusual devices or locations have accessed your account.

3. **Set a Strong Password:** Ensure your Google account has a strong password that includes letters, numbers, and symbols. Avoid using easily guessed information like birthdays or names.

**Tip:** Google's Security Checkup tool can help you review your security settings and ensure your account is protected.

## Conclusion

Staying safe and protecting your privacy on your Android phone involves taking a proactive approach to security. From setting up a secure lock screen to using two-factor authentication and managing app permissions, there are many steps you can take to keep your personal data secure. By following these best practices, you can enjoy the full benefits of your Android phone while keeping your information safe from threats

# CHAPTER 15: TROUBLESHOOTING COMMON ISSUES

Even with their advanced technology, Android phones can sometimes experience issues, whether it's an app not working correctly, the phone freezing, or connectivity problems. Fortunately, many of these issues can be resolved with simple troubleshooting steps. In this chapter, we'll guide you through diagnosing and fixing common Android phone problems, so you can get back to using your device without frustration.

## 1. Phone Running Slowly

Over time, your Android phone may begin to slow down due to various factors such as too many apps running, low storage space, or background processes. Luckily, there are several steps you can take to speed up your device.

**Steps to Improve Performance:**

1. **Close Unused Apps:** Having too many apps open at once can slow down your phone. To close them:
   - Tap the Recent Apps button (usually a square icon) or swipe up from the bottom of the screen to view your recent apps.
   - Swipe up or tap the X to close apps you're not using.

2. **Clear Cached Data:**
   - Go to Settings > Storage.

- Tap Cached Data and confirm to clear the cache. This removes temporary files that can slow down your phone.

3. **Free Up Storage Space:**
   - If your phone's storage is nearly full, it can affect performance. Go to Settings > Storage and delete unused apps, large files, or old photos and videos.
   - Use Google Photos or cloud storage to back up media and free up space.

4. **Restart Your Phone:** A simple restart can clear temporary glitches and free up resources. Press and hold the Power button, then tap Restart.

**Tip:** Regularly restarting your phone and keeping it free of unnecessary files can help prevent slowdowns.

---

## 2. Battery Draining Quickly

A common complaint among smartphone users is fast battery drain. This can be caused by power-hungry apps, high screen brightness, or background processes.

**Steps to Improve Battery Life:**

1. **Check Battery Usage:**
   - Go to Settings > Battery > Battery Usage to see which apps are consuming the most power.
   - If an app is using excessive battery, consider restricting its background activity or uninstalling it if you don't need it.

2. **Adjust Screen Brightness:**
   - Lower your screen brightness by swiping down the notification panel and adjusting the brightness slider. Alternatively, go to Settings > Display > Brightness.
   - Enable Adaptive Brightness to allow your

**phone to automatically adjust brightness based on ambient light.**

3. **Turn Off Unused Features:**
   - Disable Wi-Fi, Bluetooth, and GPS when not in use. These features can drain your battery if they are constantly scanning for connections.
   - **Swipe down the notification panel and tap the Wi-Fi, Bluetooth, or Location icons to turn them off.**

4. **Enable Battery Saver Mode:**
   - Go to Settings > Battery and turn on Battery Saver Mode to limit background processes and extend battery life.

5. **Update Apps:** Sometimes outdated apps cause unnecessary battery drain. Open the Google Play Store, tap Menu > My Apps & Games, and update any apps with available updates.

**Tip:** If your phone's battery life suddenly drops after installing a new app, try uninstalling the app to see if the battery performance improves.

---

### 3. Connectivity Problems (Wi-Fi, Bluetooth, Mobile Data)

Connectivity issues with Wi-Fi, Bluetooth, or mobile data can be frustrating, but there are several steps you can take to troubleshoot these problems.

**Wi-Fi Issues:**

1. **Toggle Wi-Fi Off and On:**
   - Swipe down the notification panel and tap the Wi-Fi icon to turn it off, wait a few seconds, then turn it back on.

2. **Restart Your Router:** If the Wi-Fi connection issue persists, try restarting your Wi-Fi router.

3. **Forget and Reconnect to the Network:**

- ∘ Go to Settings > Connections > Wi-Fi.
- ∘ **Tap and hold the network name, then select Forget Network.**
- ∘ **Reconnect by selecting the network again and entering the password.**

4. **Check for Software Updates:** Outdated software can sometimes cause Wi-Fi issues. Make sure your phone's software is up to date (see Chapter 14 for instructions on updating your phone).

**Bluetooth Issues:**

1. **Turn Bluetooth Off and On:**
   - ∘ Swipe down the notification panel and tap the Bluetooth icon to turn it off, wait a few seconds, and then turn it back on.

2. **Forget and Re-Pair Devices:**
   - ∘ Go to Settings > Connections > Bluetooth.
   - ∘ **Tap the device you're having trouble with, select Unpair, then re-pair by tapping the device name again.**

3. **Restart Your Phone:** Restart your phone to clear any temporary glitches that might be affecting Bluetooth connections.

**Mobile Data Issues:**

1. **Toggle Airplane Mode:** Sometimes switching Airplane Mode on and off resets mobile data. Swipe down from the top of the screen, tap the Airplane Mode icon to turn it on, wait a few seconds, then tap it again to turn it off.

2. **Reset Network Settings:**
   - ∘ If mobile data is still not working, go to Settings > System > Reset Options and choose Reset Network Settings. This will reset all network-related settings without affecting your apps or

personal data.

**Tip:** Check with your mobile carrier to ensure there are no service outages or issues with your data plan if mobile data problems persist.

## 4. Apps Crashing or Not Responding

Sometimes, apps may crash or freeze unexpectedly. This can be caused by issues such as bugs, corrupted cache, or outdated app versions.

Steps to Fix App Crashes:

1. **Force Stop the App:**
   - Go to Settings > Apps.
   - **Select the app that's causing issues and tap Force Stop. Reopen the app to see if the problem is resolved.**

2. **Clear App Cache and Data:**
   - Go to Settings > Apps.
   - **Select the problematic app, tap Storage, then tap Clear Cache. If the issue persists, tap Clear Data (note that clearing data may reset the app's settings and login information).**

3. **Update the App:**
   - Open the Google Play Store and search for the app. If an update is available, tap Update to install it.

4. **Reinstall the App:**
   - If the app continues to crash, uninstall it by going to Settings > Apps, selecting the app, and tapping Uninstall. Reinstall the app from the Google Play Store.

**Tip:** Always ensure your apps are updated to the latest version to avoid compatibility issues or bugs that could cause crashes.

## 5. Phone Freezing or Crashing

If your phone freezes or crashes frequently, it could be due to software glitches, insufficient storage, or app conflicts.

### Steps to Fix a Freezing or Crashing Phone:

1. **Restart Your Phone:**
   - Press and hold the Power button and tap Restart to reboot your phone. If your phone is completely unresponsive, press and hold the Power button for 10 seconds to force a restart.

2. **Check for Software Updates:**
   - Go to Settings > System > Software Update to check if an update is available. Updating your software can resolve many bugs and stability issues.

3. **Free Up Storage Space:**
   - Go to Settings > Storage and delete unnecessary files, apps, or media to free up storage. A lack of storage can cause your phone to slow down or crash.

4. **Factory Reset (as a last resort):**
   - If nothing else works and your phone continues to crash, a factory reset can restore it to its original settings, removing any software glitches. Before proceeding, ensure you've backed up all your important data.
   - **Go to Settings > System > Reset Options and choose Factory Data Reset.**

**Tip:** Factory reset should only be used as a last resort. Always back up your data before performing a reset.

---

## 6. Overheating Issues

Phones can sometimes get hot when running too many apps, charging, or in hot environments. While mild heat is normal, overheating can affect your phone's performance and battery life.

**Steps to Prevent Overheating:**

1. **Close Unnecessary Apps:**
   - Go to Recent Apps (swipe up or tap the square icon) and close apps you're not using.

2. **Avoid Heavy Usage While Charging:**
   - Using your phone for resource-heavy tasks like gaming or streaming videos while charging can generate more heat. Try to avoid this.

3. **Turn Off Unused Features:**
   - Disable Bluetooth, GPS, or mobile data when you're not using them to reduce the strain on your phone's processor.

4. **Use Your Phone in a Cool Environment:**
   - Avoid exposing your phone to direct sunlight or placing it on hot surfaces. If your phone becomes too hot, turn it off and let it cool down before using it again.

**Tip:** If your phone regularly overheats, check for app updates or consider uninstalling apps that may be using too much processing power.

---

## Conclusion

While Android phones are powerful and reliable devices, occasional issues can arise. With the right troubleshooting steps, most problems can be easily resolved without needing professional help. Whether your phone is running slowly, experiencing connectivity issues, or having battery problems, the solutions in this chapter will help you identify and fix the most common issues. Remember to keep your phone updated, clear unused apps and data regularly, and maintain good battery practices to avoid issues in the future.

---

# CHAPTER 16: ACCESSIBILITY FEATURES FOR SENIORS

Android phones offer a wide range of accessibility features that make them easier to use, especially for seniors or individuals with visual, hearing, or mobility challenges. These features help personalize the phone's interface, making the text larger, enabling voice commands, or even turning on screen readers for easier navigation. In this chapter, we'll explore the most useful accessibility settings available on Android devices and how they can be customized to meet your specific needs.

## 1. Increasing Text Size and Display Adjustments

One of the most common adjustments seniors may need is to make the text on the phone larger and easier to read. Android allows you to increase both the text size and overall display size to ensure the screen is more legible.

**How to Increase Text Size:**

1. **Open Settings:** Swipe down from the top of the screen and tap the Settings icon (a gear).
2. **Select Display:** Scroll down and tap Display.
3. **Tap Font Size:** Adjust the slider to increase or decrease the size of the text.

4. **Preview Changes:** As you adjust the slider, you'll see a preview of how the text will appear on your screen.

### How to Adjust Display Size:

1. Open Settings: Go to Settings > Display.
2. Tap Display Size: Use the slider to make everything on your screen (including icons and text) larger or smaller.
3. Choose the Size That Fits Your Needs: Adjust until you're comfortable with the size of items on your screen.

**Tip:** For seniors who prefer bolder text, you can enable Bold Text in some Android devices to make letters thicker and more defined, enhancing readability.

---

## 2. Magnification: Zooming in on Your Screen

The Magnification feature allows you to zoom in on parts of the screen for a closer look at text, images, or any on-screen content. This is particularly useful when reading small text or viewing detailed information.

### How to Enable Magnification:

1. **Open Settings:** Go to Settings > Accessibility.
2. **Tap Magnification:** Tap Magnification under the Accessibility menu.
3. **Enable Magnification Shortcut:** Toggle on the Magnification Shortcut. This adds a small icon to your screen that you can tap when you want to zoom in.

### How to Use Magnification:

- **Triple Tap:** After enabling magnification, you can triple-tap the screen to zoom in on a specific area. Use two fingers to move around the screen and pinch to zoom in or out further.
- **Magnification Button:** On some devices, a magnification icon (like a small magnifying glass) will appear at the bottom corner of the screen. Tap this icon to zoom in or out as needed.

**Tip:** Magnification is especially helpful when viewing small text in apps or websites that don't allow font size adjustments.

## 3. Voice Commands and Google Assistant

For seniors who find typing difficult or prefer to use voice commands, Android offers powerful voice control through Google Assistant. You can use your voice to make calls, send texts, search the web, or even control smart home devices.

**How to Set Up and Use Google Assistant:**

1. **Activate Google Assistant:** Hold the Home button (or swipe up from the bottom of the screen) and say, "Hey Google" or "OK Google" to activate Google Assistant.

2. **Ask for Help:** Once activated, you can ask Google Assistant for help by saying things like:

   - "Call John" (to make a phone call).
   - "Send a message to Sarah" (to send a text).
   - "Set a reminder for 3 PM" (to schedule a reminder).
   - "What's the weather like today?" (for weather updates).

**Customizing Google Assistant:**

- Open the Google Assistant settings by saying, "Open Google Assistant settings" and adjust how you interact with the assistant, such as enabling voice activation or setting reminders.

**Tip:** For seniors with limited mobility, Google Assistant can be a great way to perform tasks without needing to type or navigate menus.

## 4. Screen Readers: TalkBack for the Visually Impaired

For those with limited or no vision, Android includes TalkBack, a screen reader that reads aloud everything on the screen, including text, icons, and buttons. This allows visually impaired users to navigate their phones using touch and voice feedback.

**How to Enable TalkBack:**

1. **Open Settings**: Go to Settings > Accessibility.
2. **Select TalkBack:** Tap TalkBack and toggle it on.
3. **Follow the On-Screen Instructions:** You'll be guided through a tutorial on how to use TalkBack's gestures and controls.

**How TalkBack Works:**

- **Touch Navigation:** When TalkBack is on, you can swipe across the screen, and the phone will read aloud whatever you're touching. Double-tap to select items.
- **Swipe Gestures:** Learn specific gestures (like swiping left or right) to navigate through the phone's interface.

**Tip:** TalkBack can be overwhelming at first, so take your time learning the basic gestures. You can adjust the speech rate and verbosity in the TalkBack settings to make the voice slower or provide more detail.

---

### 5. Hearing Accessibility: Sound Amplifiers and Subtitles

For seniors with hearing impairments, Android offers a range of features to enhance sound and enable easier listening or viewing. These include Sound Amplifier, Captions, and Hearing Aid Compatibility.

**Using Sound Amplifier:**

1. **Open Settings:** Go to Settings > Accessibility.
2. **Select Sound Amplifier:** Tap Sound Amplifier and toggle it on.
3. **Connect Headphones:** Sound Amplifier works best with headphones. It enhances quiet sounds and reduces loud background noise, making it easier to hear conversations or videos.

**Enabling Captions (Subtitles):**

1. **Open Settings:** Go to Settings > Accessibility.
2. **Select Captions Preferences:** Toggle on Captions (also known as Live Caption on some devices).
3. **Customize Captions:** Choose text size, colour, and background for better visibility.

**Hearing Aid Compatibility:**

- If you use hearing aids, some Android phones support direct connectivity with Bluetooth-enabled hearing aids. Go to Settings > Connected Devices > Pair New Device to connect your hearing aid.

**Tip:** Always use high-quality wired or Bluetooth headphones for the best audio experience with Sound Amplifier.

---

## 6. Interaction and Dexterity Features

For seniors with limited dexterity or mobility challenges, Android provides features like Assistant Menu, Switch Access, and Touch & Hold Delay to make interacting with the phone easier.

**Using the Assistant Menu:** The Assistant Menu adds a floating icon to your screen that provides shortcuts to important functions, such as taking screenshots, adjusting volume, or locking the phone—helpful if you find it difficult to press buttons.

1. **Open Settings:** Go to Settings > Accessibility > Interaction and Dexterity.
2. **Enable Assistant Menu:** Toggle on Assistant Menu to place an accessible control icon on the screen.

**Using Switch Access:** Switch Access allows you to control your phone with external devices, such as switches or keyboards, which can be a helpful tool for seniors with severe mobility issues.

1. **Open Settings:** Go to Settings > Accessibility.
2. **Tap Switch Access:** Enable Switch Access and connect external switches or use the phone's buttons to control the interface.

**Adjusting Touch & Hold Delay:** If you find that the phone reacts too quickly or slowly to your touches, you can adjust the Touch & Hold Delay to customize how long you need to press before the phone registers the action.

1. **Open Settings:** Go to Settings > Accessibility > Touch & Hold Delay.
2. **Adjust Delay Time:** Choose a shorter or longer delay time based on your comfort level.

---

**7. Enhancing Visibility: High Contrast and Colour Adjustment**

Android offers several features to improve visibility for those with visual impairments or colour blindness. These settings include High Contrast Text, Colour Inversion, and Colour Correction.

**Enabling High Contrast Text:**

1. **Open Settings:** Go to Settings > Accessibility > Text and Display.
2. **Enable High Contrast Text:** Toggle on High Contrast Text to make text more visible against backgrounds.

**Using Colour Inversion:** Colour inversion swaps colours on your screen, turning light backgrounds dark and dark text light. This can be easier on the eyes, especially in low-light settings.

1. **Open Settings:** Go to Settings > Accessibility > Text and Display.
2. **Enable Colour Inversion**: Toggle Colour Inversion on to switch the colours.

**Colour Correction for Colour Blindness:** If you have colour blindness, you can adjust your screen to correct certain colours.

1. **Open Settings:** Go to Settings > Accessibility > Colour Correction.
2. **Enable Colour Correction:** Toggle it on and choose the correction mode that fits your needs, such as red-green or blue-yellow colour blindness.

**Tip:** High contrast and colour correction can help make the phone easier to read, especially for users with visual impairments or sensitivity to bright colours.

## 8. Setting Up Emergency SOS Features

For seniors who may need to call for help quickly, Android phones offer Emergency SOS and Medical Information features that allow you to send emergency alerts or make it easier for first responders to access important health information.

**Setting Up Emergency SOS:**

1. **Open Settings:** Go to Settings > Safety & Emergency or Advanced Features (depending on your phone model).

2. **Enable Emergency SOS:** Toggle on Emergency SOS. You can configure it to automatically call emergency services when you press the Power button several times in a row.

3. **Set Emergency Contacts:** Choose emergency contacts who will receive an alert when SOS is activated.

**Setting Medical Information:**

1. **Open Settings:** Go to Settings > Safety & Emergency > Medical Info.

2. **Add Medical Information:** Enter important information, such as allergies, medications, blood type, and emergency contact details. This information will be accessible from the lock screen in case of an emergency.

**Tip:** Adding emergency contacts and medical info ensures quick access for first responders, even when your phone is locked.

## Conclusion

Android offers a variety of accessibility features designed to make using your phone easier and more comfortable, particularly for seniors. Whether you need to enlarge text, use voice commands, or enable features like TalkBack or Sound Amplifier, you can customize your phone to meet your unique needs. By exploring and activating these tools, you can enjoy a more user-friendly experience, no matter your level of ability.

.

# CHAPTER 17: MANAGING STORAGE AND FILES

As you use your Android phone over time, it's easy for storage to fill up with apps, photos, videos, downloads, and system files. If your storage is full, it can slow down your phone and make it difficult to install new apps or save new data. Fortunately, Android phones come with tools to help you manage storage, delete unnecessary files, and keep your data organized. In this chapter, we'll explore how to check storage usage, clear up space, and manage files to ensure your phone runs smoothly.

## 1. Checking Your Storage Usage

The first step in managing your storage is understanding how much space you have and what's taking up the most room on your device. Android phones allow you to view detailed information about your storage, including how much space is used by apps, photos, videos, and other files.

**How to Check Your Storage:**

1. **Open Settings:** Swipe down from the top of the screen and tap the Settings icon (a gear).
2. **Select Storage:** Scroll down and tap Storage.
3. **View Storage Breakdown:** You'll see a breakdown of your storage usage, including categories like Apps, Photos & Videos, Audio, Downloads, and System. You can tap each category for more details.

**Tip:** If you notice that certain categories are taking up too much space, you can focus on clearing files from those areas first.

## 2. Freeing Up Space: Deleting Unnecessary Files

When your phone is running low on storage, one of the quickest ways to free up space is by deleting files and apps that you no longer need. This includes old photos, videos, large downloads, and unused apps.

### How to Free Up Space:

1. **Open Settings > Storage:** Go to Storage in the Settings app to see a list of categories taking up space.

2. **Use Storage Management Tools:**
   - **Free Up Space Option:** Some Android phones offer a Free Up Space button, which automatically recommends files to delete, such as unused apps, large files, or old photos.
   - **Clear Cache: Tap Cached Data and confirm to delete it. This will remove temporary files that apps use to speed up performance but aren't essential.**

3. **Manually Delete Unnecessary Files:**
   - Go to Downloads to review old files or documents you no longer need.
   - **Open the Gallery or Google Photos to delete duplicate or blurry photos and long videos you no longer need.**

**Tip:** Google Photos offers a Free Up Space feature that automatically deletes local copies of photos and videos after they've been backed up to the cloud, freeing up storage on your phone.

## 3. Managing Apps: Uninstalling and Disabling

Apps can take up a significant amount of storage space, especially if you have apps you rarely or never use. You can free up storage by uninstalling unused apps or disabling pre-installed apps that you don't need.

**How to Uninstall Apps:**

1. **Open Settings > Apps:** Go to Settings and tap Apps & Notifications (or just Apps, depending on your phone model).

2. **Select an App:** Tap the app you want to remove.

3. **Tap Uninstall:** If you no longer use the app, tap Uninstall to remove it from your device. This will delete the app and all of its data.

**Disabling Pre-Installed Apps:**

- Some apps that come pre-installed on your phone (like manufacturer-specific apps) cannot be uninstalled, but you can disable them to free up space.

  1. Open Settings > Apps and select the app.

  2. Tap Disable. This prevents the app from running and using storage space for updates or background activity.

**Tip**: Periodically review your apps and remove any that you don't use frequently to keep your storage under control.

---

### 4. Moving Files to Cloud Storage

Cloud storage services, like Google Drive, Google Photos, and Dropbox, allow you to store your photos, videos, documents, and other files in the cloud rather than on your phone. This helps free up local storage and ensures your important files are backed up.

**Using Google Photos for Cloud Storage:**

1. **Open Google Photos:** If it's not installed, download it from the Google Play Store.

2. **Enable Backup & Sync:** Tap your profile icon (top-right corner), go to Photos Settings > Backup & Sync, and turn it on. This will automatically upload your photos and videos to your Google account.

3. **Free Up Space:** After your media is backed up, tap the Free Up Space button in Google Photos to delete local copies from your phone.

## Using Google Drive for Files:

1. **Open Google Drive:** Download Google Drive from the Play Store if it's not installed.

2. **Upload Files:** Tap the plus (+) icon and select Upload. Choose the files or folders you want to store in the cloud.

3. **Access Files from Anywhere:** Once uploaded, you can access these files from any device by signing in to your Google account.

**Tip:** Cloud storage services offer free storage with limited space (Google Photos offers 15 GB free with Google Drive), but you can purchase additional storage if needed.

---

## 5. Managing Files with the Files App

Android includes a built-in Files app that makes it easy to organize and manage the files stored on your phone. You can use the app to view, move, delete, or share files such as documents, photos, videos, and downloads.

## How to Use the Files App:

1. **Open the Files App:** Depending on your phone model, the app may be called Files by Google or simply Files. You can find it in your app drawer or by searching for it.

2. **Browse Your Files:** The Files app categorizes your data into sections like Downloads, Images, Videos, Audio, and Documents. Tap a category to browse your files.

3. **Delete or Move Files:**

   ◦ **Delete Files:** Select a file, tap the three-dot menu, and choose Delete to remove it from your phone.

   ◦ **Move Files: You can move files between different folders or storage locations (like your**

**SD card or internal storage) by selecting the file and tapping Move or Copy.**

**Tip:** The Files app also has a clean-up tool that suggests files you can delete, such as large files, duplicate files, or temporary files.

## 6. Using an SD Card for Extra Storage

Many Android phones allow you to expand your storage by adding an SD card. An SD card can be used to store apps, photos, videos, and other files, freeing up your phone's internal storage.

**How to Use an SD Card:**

1. **Insert the SD Card:** Locate the SD card slot on your phone (usually next to the SIM card slot) and insert the SD card.

2. **Set SD Card as Default Storage:**
   - Go to Settings > Storage.
   - **Tap the SD card and choose Format as Internal if you want to use the SD card as your main storage. This will move some apps and files to the SD card automatically.**

3. **Move Apps to SD Card:**
   - Some apps can be moved to the SD card to free up internal storage. Go to Settings > Apps, select an app, and tap Move to SD Card if the option is available.
   - **Note that some apps, especially system apps, cannot be moved to the SD card.**

**Tip:** When purchasing an SD card, make sure it's compatible with your phone and has enough storage capacity to meet your needs (32 GB, 64 GB, or more).

## 7. Managing Downloads and Media Files

Downloads and media files (like photos, videos, and music) can quickly take up space on your phone. It's a good idea to regularly check your Downloads folder and delete files you no longer need.

**Managing Downloads:**

1. **Open the Files App:** Go to the Files or Downloads app on your phone.

2. Review Downloaded Files: Check for files you've downloaded, such as PDFs, images, or APKs, that you no longer need.

3. **Delete Unnecessary Files:** Tap the file, select the three-dot menu, and choose Delete to remove it from your phone.

## Managing Photos and Videos:

- Use the Gallery or Google Photos app to organize your media. You can delete blurry photos, old screenshots, or duplicate pictures to save space.

- Transfer media to your computer or cloud storage regularly to free up storage.

**Tip:** Set Google Photos to automatically back up and sync your photos and videos to Google Drive. Once synced, use the Free Up Space option to delete local copies from your phone.

---

## 8. Backing Up and Restoring Your Data

Backing up your data ensures that if anything happens to your phone, your important files, apps, and settings can be restored. Android offers built-in tools to back up data automatically to Google Drive.

## How to Back Up Your Data:

1. **Open Settings > System > Backup:** Go to the Backup section in your phone's settings.

2. **Enable Google Backup:** Turn on Backup to Google Drive. This will automatically back up your app data, contacts, device settings, and more to your Google account.

3. **Check Backup Settings:** Review what's being backed up by tapping on Backed-up Account. Make sure important items, like your contacts and photos, are included.

## Restoring Your Data:

- If you switch to a new phone or reset your device, you can restore your backed-up data by signing into your Google account during the setup process. Your apps, settings, and other data will be downloaded from your backup.

**Tip:** Regular backups can save you time and stress if you ever need to reset your phone or switch to a new device.

## Conclusion

Managing your storage and files is essential for keeping your Android phone running smoothly and ensuring that you have enough space for new apps, photos, and data. By regularly checking your storage, deleting unnecessary files, using cloud storage or SD cards, and taking advantage of Android's built-in file management tools, you can keep your phone organized and free from clutter. Whether you're freeing up space, backing up your data, or moving apps to an SD card, these strategies will help you get the most out of your Android phone

# CHAPTER 18: USING YOUR PHONE FOR ENTERTAINMENT

Your Android phone is a powerful entertainment device that offers a variety of ways to relax and enjoy your favourite hobbies. Whether you're into music, movies, games, or books, your phone can provide endless entertainment at your fingertips. In this chapter, we'll explore how to use your phone for entertainment, covering everything from streaming music and videos to gaming and reading e-books. With the right apps and settings, you can turn your phone into your personal entertainment hub.

## 1. Streaming Music

One of the most popular ways to use your phone for entertainment is by streaming music. There are numerous music apps available on Android, allowing you to access millions of songs, albums, and playlists from your favourite artists. Whether you want to listen to curated playlists, discover new music, or play your own library, your phone has it all.

**Popular Music Streaming Apps:**

- **Spotify:** One of the most widely used music streaming services, Spotify offers access to millions of songs, curated playlists, and personalized recommendations. You can create your own playlists, listen to podcasts, and discover new music through the app.

- **YouTube Music:** If you enjoy music videos along with

your songs, YouTube Music offers both audio tracks and music videos. You can watch official music videos, live performances, and more while listening to your favourite tunes.

- **Apple Music:** Although originally designed for iOS, Apple Music is available on Android as well. It gives you access to an extensive music library, curated playlists, and exclusive content.
- **Pandora:** Known for its personalized radio stations, Pandora creates radio-like playlists based on your favourite genres, artists, or songs.

## How to Stream Music on Your Phone:

1. **Download the App:** Go to the Google Play Store and download a music streaming app like Spotify, YouTube Music, or Apple Music.
2. **Sign Up or Log In:** Create an account or log in if you already have one.
3. **Search for Music:** Use the search bar to find your favourite artists, albums, or genres.
4. **Create Playlists**: Most music apps allow you to create custom playlists for different moods or occasions.
5. **Listen Offline:** With a premium subscription, many apps allow you to download music for offline listening, so you don't need an internet connection to enjoy your songs.

**Tip:** Use Bluetooth or wired headphones for the best audio experience, or connect your phone to a speaker for shared listening.

## 2. Watching Movies and TV Shows

Your Android phone is perfect for streaming movies and TV shows on the go or from the comfort of your home. With various streaming services available, you can watch thousands of shows, films, and documentaries whenever you want.

**Popular Video Streaming Apps:**

- **Netflix:** One of the most popular streaming services, Netflix offers a vast library of movies, TV series, and documentaries across all genres.
- **Amazon Prime Video:** With Amazon Prime Video, you can watch exclusive TV shows, movies, and Amazon Originals. It also offers a variety of rentals and purchases for new releases.
- **Disney+:** Ideal for families and Disney fans, Disney+ offers a large collection of Disney classics, Pixar films, Marvel movies, Star Wars, and more.
- **YouTube:** Beyond music videos, YouTube has a wide range of free and paid content, including movies, shows, and user-created videos.

## How to Stream Movies and Shows:

1. **Download a Streaming App:** Visit the Google Play Store and download apps like Netflix, Amazon Prime Video, or Disney+.
2. **Sign In or Create an Account:** Log in or sign up for a subscription if necessary.
3. **Browse for Content:** Search or browse through categories to find movies or shows to watch.
4. **Watch Offline:** Many streaming apps allow you to download shows and movies for offline viewing, ideal for travel or areas with poor connectivity.

**Tip:** Watching movies in landscape mode provides a more immersive experience. You can also cast your phone's screen to a TV using Google Chromecast or a compatible smart TV.

## 3. Playing Mobile Games

Mobile gaming has come a long way, and your Android phone is capable of running both casual and advanced games. Whether you prefer puzzle games, action-packed shooters, or strategy games, there's something for everyone on the Google Play Store.

**Types of Mobile Games:**

- **Puzzle and Brain Games:** Games like Candy Crush Saga, Words with Friends, and Sudoku are great for casual gamers who enjoy puzzles and challenges.
- **Action and Adventure Games:** For a more immersive experience, try action-adventure games like Fortnite, PUBG Mobile, or Call of Duty Mobile, which feature intense multiplayer gameplay.
- **Strategy and Simulation Games:** Games like Clash of Clans, SimCity BuildIt, and Rise of Kingdoms allow you to build cities, plan strategies, and conquer new lands.
- **Casino and Card Games:** If you enjoy card games, Solitaire, Texas Hold'em Poker, and Blackjack offer great digital versions for entertainment.

**How to Download and Play Mobile Games:**

1. **Open the Google Play Store:** Search for games in the Games section or type the name of the game you want to download.
2. **Install the Game:** Tap Install to download the game to your phone.
3. **Start Playing:** Open the game from your home screen and follow the in-game tutorial to get started.

**Tip:** Some games require an internet connection, but many also offer offline modes for gaming without data usage. Check the game's description to see if offline play is available.

---

### 4. Reading E-books and Audiobooks

For book lovers, Android phones can double as portable e-readers or audiobook players. Whether you enjoy novels, nonfiction, or magazines, you can access an extensive library of e-books and audiobooks.

**Popular Reading and Audiobook Apps:**

- **Amazon Kindle:** The Kindle app offers access to millions of e-books and audiobooks. You can adjust text size, background colour, and brightness for a comfortable reading experience.

- **Google Play Books:** Google's own Play Books app allows you to purchase and read e-books and listen to audiobooks across a variety of genres.
- **Audible:** Known for its large audiobook library, Audible provides access to audiobooks, narrated by professional voice actors and authors themselves.
- **Libby:** If you prefer borrowing books, Libby connects to your local library to let you borrow e-books and audiobooks for free with a library card.

**How to Use Your Phone for Reading:**

1. **Download a Reading App:** Install Kindle, Google Play Books, or another reading app from the Google Play Store.
2. **Buy or Borrow Books:** Purchase e-books or audiobooks from the app, or connect to your library account in apps like Libby to borrow them for free.
3. **Adjust Reading Preferences:** Customize the font size, screen brightness, and background colour to make reading more comfortable.
4. **Listen to Audiobooks:** For audiobooks, simply plug in headphones or connect to a speaker and enjoy a hands-free listening experience.

**Tip:** Many apps, like Google Play Books and Kindle, offer night mode, which makes the screen easier on the eyes during low-light conditions.

---

## 5. Watching YouTube and Other Online Videos

Besides streaming services, YouTube is one of the most popular platforms for watching a wide range of video content, from educational tutorials to vlogs, news, and user-generated content. You can also use other video platforms like Vimeo, Twitch, and TikTok for specific types of videos and live streams.

**How to Use YouTube for Entertainment:**

1. **Download the YouTube App:** If it's not already installed, download YouTube from the Google Play Store.

2. **Sign In to YouTube:** You can use your Google account to sign in and subscribe to your favourite channels.

3. **Search for Videos:** Use the Search bar to find videos on any topic of interest, whether it's music, cooking tutorials, travel vlogs, or product reviews.

4. **Subscribe to Channels:** Subscribe to your favourite YouTube channels to receive updates on new videos.

5. **Watch Offline:** With a YouTube Premium subscription, you can download videos to watch offline, making it a great option for travel or commuting.

**Tip:** YouTube also allows you to create custom playlists of your favourite videos so you can quickly access them whenever you want.

## 6. Listening to Podcasts

Podcasts are an increasingly popular way to stay informed and entertained. Whether you enjoy news, storytelling, interviews, or educational content, there are podcasts for every interest.

**Popular Podcast Apps:**

- **Google Podcasts:** Google's own podcast app allows you to subscribe to your favourite shows and discover new podcasts across a wide variety of topics.

- **Spotify:** In addition to music, Spotify offers a large selection of podcasts, from true crime to business, comedy, and health.

- **Pocket Casts:** A dedicated podcast app, Pocket Casts lets you manage your subscriptions, create playlists, and download episodes for offline listening.

**How to Listen to Podcasts:**

1. **Download a Podcast App:** Install Google Podcasts, Spotify, or Pocket Casts from the Play Store.

2. **Search for Podcasts:** Use the app's search bar to find podcasts on topics you're interested in.

3. **Subscribe:** Subscribe to shows so that new episodes automatically download to your phone.

4. **Listen Offline:** Most podcast apps allow you to download episodes for offline listening, which is perfect for when you're on the go.

**Tip:** Use the sleep timer feature in podcast apps if you like to fall asleep while listening to your favourite shows. This automatically stops playback after a set time.

## Conclusion

Your Android phone is a versatile entertainment device, capable of keeping you engaged with music, movies, games, books, and more. With the wide range of apps available, you can customize your entertainment experience to suit your interests and preferences, whether you're at home or on the go. By exploring the different streaming, reading, gaming, and video options, you can turn your phone into a powerful entertainment hub that fits perfectly into your lifestyle.

# CHAPTER 19: STAYING CONNECTED WITH SOCIAL MEDIA

Social media has become a central part of modern life, making it easier than ever to stay connected with friends, family, and communities across the globe. Whether you want to share updates, photos, or keep in touch with loved ones, your Android phone offers access to a variety of social media apps that can help you do just that. In this chapter, we'll explore how to get started with social media, manage your privacy settings, and make the most of popular platforms like Facebook, Instagram, Twitter, and WhatsApp.

## 1. Getting Started with Social Media on Android

Before diving into specific apps, it's important to understand the basics of social media and how it works. Social media platforms allow you to create a profile, connect with other users, and share content such as posts, photos, videos, and updates. Each platform has its own unique features, but the overall goal is to keep people connected and engaged with their communities.

**How to Install Social Media Apps:**

1. **Open Google Play Store:** On your Android phone, open the Google Play Store.

2. **Search for Social Media Apps:** Use the search bar to find the apps you want to install (e.g., Facebook, Instagram, Twitter, WhatsApp).

3. **Install the Apps:** Tap Install to download the app to your phone. Once the installation is complete, you'll find the app on your home screen or in the app drawer.

4. **Sign Up or Log In:** Open the app and sign up for a new account or log in if you already have an account.

**Tip:** Most social media platforms require an email address or phone number to create an account. Make sure to use a secure password when signing up.

## 2. Facebook: Connecting with Friends and Family

Facebook is one of the largest social media platforms in the world and is popular among people of all ages. It allows you to share updates, photos, and videos, and interact with friends, family, and communities through posts, comments, and messages.

**Key Features of Facebook:**

- **News Feed:** This is where you'll see updates from your friends, family, and pages you follow. You can scroll through posts, like them, comment, or share them with others.

- **Profile:** Your personal profile is where you can share information about yourself, such as your location, job, hobbies, and interests. It also includes a timeline of your posts, photos, and life events.

- **Messenger:** Facebook has a separate app called Messenger for private messages and video calls. This is a great way to chat with friends or have group conversations.

- **Groups and Pages:** Facebook allows you to join groups based on shared interests (such as hobbies or local communities) or follow pages of your favourite brands, public figures, or organizations.

**How to Use Facebook:**

1. **Post an Update:** Tap the What's on your mind? box at the top of your News Feed to share a status update. You can

add text, photos, videos, or even check in to a location.

2. **Like, Comment, and Share:** Interact with posts by tapping Like, leaving a comment, or tapping Share to share the post with your friends.

3. **Send a Message:** Use Messenger to send private messages to friends. You can also make voice or video calls through the Messenger app.

**Tip:** Facebook is a great platform for keeping up with family and friends, but it's important to regularly review your privacy settings to ensure your personal information is shared only with the people you trust.

---

### 3. Instagram: Sharing Photos and Videos

Instagram is a social media platform primarily focused on sharing photos and videos. It's a fun way to stay visually connected with friends and family, as well as to follow interesting accounts related to hobbies, travel, food, and more.

**Key Features of Instagram:**

- **Photo and Video Sharing:** You can upload photos or videos from your camera roll or take them directly within the app to share with your followers.

- **Stories:** Instagram Stories allows you to post temporary photos or videos that disappear after 24 hours. Stories can include stickers, text, and filters for a creative touch.

- **Direct Messaging:** You can send private messages, photos, and videos to individuals or groups through Instagram's Direct Messages (DMs).

- **Explore:** The Explore section helps you discover new content based on your interests, including accounts, hashtags, and popular posts.

**How to Use Instagram:**

1. **Post a Photo or Video:** Tap the + button at the bottom of the screen to upload a photo or video. You can apply filters, add a caption, and share it with your followers.

2. **View Stories:** At the top of your Instagram feed, you'll see circles representing stories from the people you follow. Tap to view their stories, or create your own by tapping Your Story.

3. **Like and Comment:** Double-tap a photo to like it, or tap the speech bubble icon below a post to leave a comment.

**Tip:** Use Instagram's privacy settings to choose who can see your posts. You can set your account to private, meaning only approved followers can view your content.

## 4. X (Twitter): Sharing Thoughts in Real-Time

X is a platform where users share short messages called tweets. It's a great way to follow news, entertainment, and conversations in real-time. Twitter is widely used by public figures, journalists, businesses, and everyday people to share thoughts and updates quickly.

**Key Features of Twitter:**

- **Tweets:** Tweets are short messages (up to 280 characters) that you can post to share thoughts, links, photos, and videos.
- **Retweets:** You can retweet someone else's post to share it with your followers.
- **Trending Topics:** The Trending section highlights popular conversations, hashtags, and topics in real-time.
- **Following:** Instead of friending people like on Facebook, you follow other accounts to see their tweets in your timeline. You can follow friends, celebrities, news outlets, and more.

**How to Use X:**

1. **Post a Tweet:** Tap the feather icon in the bottom-right corner of the app to compose a tweet. You can add text, photos, or videos, and include hashtags (like #travel) to reach a wider audience.

2. **Like, Retweet, and Reply:** Interact with tweets by

tapping the heart to like them, tapping retweet to share them with your followers, or replying to join the conversation.

3. **Follow Accounts:** Tap the Search icon to find people, news outlets, or topics of interest. Tap Follow to start seeing their tweets in your feed.

**Tip:** X can be fast-paced, so it's helpful to follow accounts that post regularly about topics you're interested in. You can also use Twitter Lists to organize accounts into specific categories.

## 5. WhatsApp: Messaging and Video Calling

WhatsApp is a messaging app that allows you to send messages, photos, videos, and make voice or video calls—all for free using your phone's internet connection. It's an excellent option for staying in touch with friends and family, especially those who are far away.

**Key Features of WhatsApp:**

- **Text Messaging:** Send text messages to individuals or groups in real time. You can also share photos, videos, and voice messages.

- **Voice and Video Calls:** WhatsApp lets you make free voice and video calls to anyone with the app, regardless of where they are in the world.

- **Groups:** Create group chats for family, friends, or specific interests, where everyone in the group can send messages, share media, and join calls.

- **Status:** Similar to Instagram Stories, WhatsApp Status allows you to share text, photos, and videos that disappear after 24 hours.

**How to Use WhatsApp:**

1. **Set Up WhatsApp:** After installing the app, verify your phone number to set up your account.

2. **Send a Message:** Tap the chat icon in the bottom-right corner to start a new conversation. Select a contact, type

your message, and tap Send.

3. **Make a Call:** Tap the phone icon or video camera icon in a chat to make a voice or video call.

4. **Create a Group Chat:** Tap the three-dot menu and select New Group. Add participants and start chatting with everyone in the group.

**Tip:** WhatsApp uses end-to-end encryption, which means that only you and the person you're communicating with can read or listen to your messages and calls. This makes it one of the most secure messaging platforms.

## 6. Managing Privacy and Security on Social Media

While social media is a great way to stay connected, it's important to manage your privacy and security settings to protect your personal information and control who can see your posts.

**General Privacy Tips:**

- **Adjust Privacy Settings:** Most social media platforms allow you to control who can see your posts, photos, and personal information. Set your accounts to private if you only want approved friends or followers to see your content.

- **Be Careful What You Share:** Avoid posting sensitive information like your address, phone number, or financial details.

- **Use Strong Passwords:** Ensure each of your social media accounts is protected by a strong password. Consider enabling two-factor authentication (2FA) for extra security.

- **Review Friend and Follower Requests:** Only accept friend or follower requests from people you know or trust. Be wary of requests from strangers.

**How to Manage Privacy Settings:**

1. **Open the App:** Go to the social media app you want to adjust.

2. **Access Privacy Settings:** Tap on your profile icon and look for the Settings or Privacy section.

3. **Adjust Who Can See Your Posts:** In the privacy settings, you can control who can see your posts, send you messages, and tag you in photos.

**Tip:** It's a good idea to review your privacy settings every few months to ensure they still match your preferences.

## Conclusion

Social media is a powerful tool for staying connected with friends, family, and the world around you. Whether you prefer sharing photos on Instagram, catching up with loved ones on Facebook, or having real-time conversations on Twitter, there's a platform for everyone. By using the tips and guidelines in this chapter, you can make the most of social media while staying safe and maintaining control over your privacy. With your Android phone in hand, the world of social media is just a few taps away

# CHAPTER 20: THE ROLE OF AI IN ANDROID PHONES

Artificial intelligence (AI) is becoming an integral part of the Android ecosystem, transforming how we interact with our phones and making everyday tasks easier and more intuitive. AI enables Android phones to learn from user behaviour, offer personalized recommendations, automate repetitive tasks, and improve overall performance. From voice assistants and smart photography features to battery optimization and security enhancements, AI is revolutionizing the Android experience. In this chapter, we'll explore the various ways AI is used in Android phones and how it enhances your day-to-day interactions with your device.

## 1. Google Assistant: Your AI-Powered Personal Assistant

Google Assistant is perhaps the most well-known AI feature on Android phones. It's a voice-activated virtual assistant that can help you with various tasks, including making phone calls, sending messages, setting reminders, and answering questions. The power of AI allows Google Assistant to understand natural language, learn from your interactions, and offer more personalized assistance over time.

**Key Features of Google Assistant:**

- **Voice Commands:** You can activate Google Assistant by saying "Hey Google" or "OK Google." You can ask it questions, give it commands (like turning on the flashlight or setting an alarm), or ask it to perform actions (like sending a text or opening an app).

- **Smart Home Integration:** Google Assistant can control smart home devices like lights, thermostats, and security cameras. You can use voice commands to manage your smart home, making daily tasks even more convenient.

- **Personalized Suggestions:** Google Assistant learns from your habits and usage patterns to offer personalized recommendations, such as reminders to call a friend you often speak with, or suggesting directions to places you frequently visit.

**How to Use Google Assistant:**

1. **Activate Google Assistant:** Say "Hey Google" or press and hold the Home button (or swipe up from the bottom of the screen) to activate Google Assistant.

2. **Ask a Question or Give a Command:** You can ask things like, "What's the weather today?" or "Remind me to take my medicine at 8 AM."

3. **Control Apps and Settings:** Ask Google Assistant to play music, open apps, or adjust phone settings (like brightness or Wi-Fi).

**Tip:** Google Assistant gets smarter with more use, adapting to your preferences and learning your routines to provide better suggestions and responses over time.

---

### 2. AI in Photography: Smarter Cameras and Image Processing

AI has dramatically improved the camera experience on Android phones. Modern Android cameras use AI to recognize scenes, optimize settings, and even enhance photos in real-time, making it easier than ever to take professional-looking photos without needing to adjust complicated camera settings manually.

**AI-Powered Camera Features:**

- **Scene Recognition:** AI-powered cameras can automatically detect scenes (like sunsets, food, landscapes, or portraits) and adjust the camera settings to capture the best possible image for that scene.
- **Portrait Mode:** AI enhances portrait mode by identifying the subject of a photo and blurring the background to create a bokeh effect, making the subject stand out.
- **Night Mode:** AI helps capture better photos in low-light conditions by adjusting exposure settings and reducing noise in the image.
- **AI Filters and Enhancements**: Many camera apps offer AI-driven filters that automatically enhance colours, lighting, and sharpness in real-time or during post-processing.
- **Face and Object Detection:** AI-powered cameras can detect faces and objects to improve focus and exposure. This is especially helpful for group photos, where the camera ensures everyone is in focus.

**How to Use AI Camera Features:**

1. **Open the Camera App:** On most Android phones, the default camera app comes with AI features built-in.
2. **Use Auto Mode:** In Auto Mode, AI will automatically detect scenes and apply the best settings for you.
3. **Explore AI-Powered Features:** Look for options like Night Mode, Portrait Mode, or AI Filters to improve your photos with minimal effort.

**Tip:** Many Android phones, especially those from manufacturers like Samsung, Google, and Huawei, come with AI-enhanced photography features. Experiment with these modes to capture better images without the need for manual adjustments.

## 3. AI-Powered Battery Optimization

One of the most practical applications of AI in Android phones is battery management. AI helps optimize battery usage by learning how you use your phone and making adjustments to prolong battery life. It can manage background processes, adjust settings based on your habits, and suggest power-saving options.

**AI Battery Features:**

- **Adaptive Battery:** This feature uses AI to monitor which apps you use the most and which ones you rarely open. It then limits background activity for less-used apps to conserve battery power.

- **Power Management Suggestions:** Android phones equipped with AI can offer suggestions for optimizing battery life based on your current usage patterns. For example, it might suggest dimming the screen brightness or turning off unused features like Bluetooth or GPS.

- **Battery Saver Mode:** AI helps manage Battery Saver Mode, which automatically limits power-hungry processes when your battery is low, extending the remaining battery life.

**How to Use AI for Battery Optimization:**

1. **Open Settings:** Go to Settings > Battery.
2. **Enable Adaptive Battery:** Look for Adaptive Battery and toggle it on. This allows AI to manage your apps and background processes more efficiently.
3. **Check Power Management Suggestions:** Occasionally, you'll see notifications with suggestions for saving battery life based on how you're using your phone. Follow these tips to maximize battery performance.

**Tip:** AI-powered battery optimization helps extend the battery life without requiring you to manually manage apps or adjust settings frequently.

---

## 4. Personalized Recommendations

AI on Android devices is also used to provide personalized recommendations for various services, from apps and content to shopping and dining suggestions. These recommendations are based on your usage patterns, location, and preferences.

**How AI Provides Recommendations:**

- **Google Play Store:** AI suggests apps, games, movies, and books based on what you've previously downloaded or interacted with. The more you use your phone, the more personalized the recommendations become.

- **Google Discover:** This is the personalized news feed that appears when you swipe right from your home screen. AI curates articles, videos, and news stories based on your interests and browsing habits.

- **Maps and Navigation:** Google Maps uses AI to provide personalized recommendations for nearby restaurants, stores, or attractions based on your location, the time of day, and past preferences.

- **Shopping Recommendations**: Apps like Google Search and Chrome use AI to recommend products you might be interested in based on previous searches or interactions with ads.

**How to Use Personalized Recommendations:**

1. **Explore Google Discover:** Swipe right from your home screen to see personalized news and content suggestions based on your interests.

2. **Browse the Play Store:** Open the Google Play Store to see personalized app and game recommendations in the For You section.

3. **Use Google Maps:** Open Google Maps to get personalized suggestions for nearby places to eat, shop, or visit based on your preferences and past searches.

**Tip:** AI recommendations become more accurate the more you interact with content on your phone. However, if you feel the recommendations are not relevant, you can adjust your preferences in the app settings.

## 5. AI in Security and Privacy

Android phones also use AI to enhance security and protect your privacy. AI-powered features help detect and block potential threats, keep your device secure, and manage privacy settings.

**AI-Powered Security Features:**

- **Face Unlock:** Many Android phones now use AI-powered facial recognition for Face Unlock. The AI ensures that the phone only unlocks when it detects your face, providing a secure and convenient way to access your device.

- **On-Device Machine Learning for Privacy**: Google's Android Privacy features use on-device machine learning to identify and block apps or processes that could pose a privacy risk, such as apps that attempt to track your location or access sensitive information without your consent.

- **Smart App Permissions:** AI helps manage app permissions, analysing which permissions apps request and offering suggestions on whether they are necessary. You can choose to deny or grant these permissions based on AI's recommendations.

- **Google Play Protect**: This AI-powered service scans apps on the Google Play Store and on your device for potential malware, warning you about apps that could compromise your security.

**How to Use AI Security Features:**

1. **Enable Face Unlock:** Go to Settings > Security and enable Face Unlock if your phone supports it. This feature uses AI to quickly and securely unlock your phone.

2. **Use Google Play Protect:** Open the Google Play Store, tap the menu icon, and select Play Protect to view the status of your app scans and security updates.

3. **Review App Permissions**: Go to Settings > Privacy > Permission Manager to view and manage permissions

for individual apps based on AI recommendations.

**Tip:** AI security features work quietly in the background to protect your phone, but it's a good idea to periodically review your security settings and update apps to take full advantage of the latest protections.

## 6. AI and Voice Recognition

Voice recognition powered by AI is used in more than just Google Assistant. Many Android apps and services utilize AI voice recognition to improve accessibility and convenience, allowing you to control your phone or input text using only your voice.

**Uses of AI Voice Recognition:**

- **Voice Typing:** When composing messages, emails, or notes, you can use AI-powered voice typing to dictate text instead of typing manually. This feature recognizes your voice and converts speech to text in real time.

- **Hands-Free Commands:** AI voice recognition allows you to control certain aspects of your phone, such as making calls, sending texts, or even controlling smart home devices, all without touching your phone.

- **Voice Search:** You can use voice search in apps like Google Search, YouTube, and Maps to find information quickly and easily by speaking your query instead of typing.

**How to Use Voice Typing:**

1. **Open a Text Field:** In any app where you can type (such as Messages or Email), tap the microphone icon on your keyboard to enable voice typing.

2. **Start Dictating:** Speak your message clearly, and the phone will convert your speech to text.

**Tip:** Voice recognition works best in quiet environments. You can also adjust language and accent settings for improved accuracy.

## Conclusion

AI is transforming Android phones into smarter, more intuitive devices, helping users accomplish tasks more efficiently while enhancing overall usability. Whether you're using Google Assistant, improving your photography with AI-powered features, optimizing your battery life, or ensuring your device's security, AI plays a crucial role in making your Android phone a powerful tool. As AI continues to evolve, the capabilities of your phone will only grow, making daily interactions easier, faster, and more personalized.

# CHAPTER 21: CONCLUSION: ENJOY YOUR ANDROID EXPERIENCE

Congratulations! You've reached the end of this guide, and now you are well on your way to becoming confident in using your Android phone. Android is an incredibly versatile and powerful operating system that offers a wide range of features to make your life easier, more connected, and more enjoyable. Whether you're using your phone to keep in touch with loved ones, manage your daily tasks, explore new apps, or simply have fun, your Android phone is a tool that can fit seamlessly into your life.

---

## 1. Embracing Your Android Phone's Flexibility

One of the greatest things about Android phones is their **flexibility** and **customizability**. You've learned how to personalize your home screen, change settings to fit your needs, and explore the vast world of apps that can enhance your daily life. Whether you prefer larger text for easier reading, specific ringtones for different contacts, or customized app layouts, your Android phone can be tailored to work exactly how you like.

Throughout this guide, you've discovered:

- **How to make and receive calls** so you can stay connected with family and friends.
- **Sending text messages and emails** to share updates and

communicate easily.

- **Downloading and using apps** that make life more convenient and entertaining.
- **Managing your phone's settings** to make it more comfortable and accessible for your specific needs.
- **Staying secure** by protecting your personal information and learning safe practices.

With all of these tools and tips, your phone can become a trusted companion, helping you with everyday tasks, providing entertainment, and keeping you in touch with the people who matter most.

## 2. Staying Connected and Exploring New Features

Your Android phone is more than just a tool for making calls— it's a gateway to staying connected with the world around you. Whether it's through apps like **WhatsApp**, **Facebook**, or **Zoom**, you can video call, chat, or share moments with family and friends, no matter where they are.

There's also so much more to explore! With the **Google Play Store**, you have access to millions of apps that can help with everything from health tracking to organizing your finances, learning new skills, and staying entertained with movies, music, and games.

Don't be afraid to try new things—whether it's learning a new app, customizing your phone further, or discovering how to use more advanced features like **Google Assistant** for voice commands and smart home control.

## 3. Keeping Your Phone Updated

As you continue to use your Android phone, remember to keep it updated with the latest software releases from Android. These updates often come with improved security, new features, and optimizations that can make your phone run even better.

To check for updates, simply go to **Settings > Software Update**, and follow the instructions to install any available updates.

Regular updates will ensure that your phone stays secure and continues to work smoothly.

## 4. Troubleshooting and Help

Even with the best preparation, you may run into an occasional issue with your phone. Don't worry—Android phones come with built-in troubleshooting tools, and there are always resources available to help.

- **Settings**: Many common problems can be solved through your phone's settings. Use the **Help** section in the **Settings** menu or the **Google support website** to find solutions for common issues.
- **Google Play Store**: If an app is not working properly, try checking for updates in the **Google Play Store** or reinstalling the app.
- **Manufacturer Support**: Depending on your phone's brand (Samsung, Google, etc.), you can access support from the manufacturer's website or visit a local service center for hands-on help.

Remember, there's always a solution, and help is just a tap away.

## 5. Enjoying the Android Experience

Your Android phone is designed to be easy to use, adaptable, and fun. Now that you've explored its features and learned how to make it your own, you can continue to discover new ways to use your phone every day. Whether you're connecting with family, staying on top of your health, exploring hobbies, or simply playing games, your Android phone is there to enhance your experience and bring convenience to your daily life.

Take your time, experiment with new apps and settings, and enjoy the journey of getting to know your device better. With all the skills you've gained from this guide, your phone will become an invaluable companion, helping you navigate the modern world with confidence and ease.

## Conclusion

Thank you for taking the time to learn about your Android phone. We hope this guide has empowered you to use your device with confidence and excitement. Android phones are powerful, customizable, and endlessly useful—there's always more to explore and enjoy.

Remember, technology is here to make life easier, and your Android phone is a perfect example of that. Whether you're texting a friend, checking the news, or taking photos of special moments, your phone is there to help. Enjoy your Android experience, and don't hesitate to continue exploring all the amazing things your phone can do!

Happy exploring, and enjoy your Android journey!

www.ingramcontent.com/pod-product-compliance
Lightning Source LLC
LaVergne TN
LVHW051243050326
832903LV00028B/2545